My Dearest Diary

Five Years in the Life of
Cathy Cornellia
1952 to 1956

By CATHY CORNELLIA

Campfire Stories Media LLC

Published by:
Campfire Stories Media LLC

Copyright © 2018 Stacey Palmer
All rights reserved.

Written By: Cathy Cornellia
Edited By: Anastasia Rose

This book contains the actual diary entries of Cathy Cornellia.
Some portions have been edited for clarity and readability.
Some names and identifying details have been changed to protect the privacy of individuals.

ISBN: 1537466240
ISBN-13: 978-1537466248

CONTENTS

Introduction: 2014 *Pg. i*

Chapter 1: 1952 *Pg. 1*

Chapter 2: 1953 *Pg. 63*

Chapter 3: 1954 *Pg. 103*

Chapter 4: 1955 *Pg. 147*

Chapter 5: 1956 *Pg. 201*

Epilogue: 2009 *Pg. 247*

Glossary *Pg. 251*

Introduction

My grandma passed away in January, 2014. A few months later, while my mom was helping take care of her things, she came upon a box that contained an empty heart-shaped candy box, some pressed flowers, a prom invitation, and a small red book with a broken lock on the side. My grandma kept journals most of her adult life, but this diary wasn't with the rest of them. This one was kept in a special place, apart from the others. She had started writing in it when she was just 13 years old. That meant that my grandma had kept those flowers and other keepsakes safe for about 60 years.

My mom read the diary and told me about some of her favorite parts. This was a side of my grandma I never knew, and I was curious to read it myself. The next time I visited my parents, I picked up the diary and started reading it after my parents went to bed. I stayed up most of the night. It was fascinating to read about how my grandparents met and fell in love, but more than that, I was surprised by how much I could relate to this young girl. She was creative, sensitive, loved easily and with her whole heart, and dreamt of what her life would be like when she grew up. It reminded me of the coming-of-age books I read when I was that age, and how important they were to me.

I shared some of the stories from the diary with my friends, and they all expressed a desire to read the rest. This gave me the initial idea to someday publish her diary for others to enjoy. My grandma had always wanted to be a writer, and in her later journals, she wrote about how she had hoped that her journals would someday help others who would read them. She had even picked out a pen name, Cathy Cornellia.

So, this is that diary, with some names changed for privacy, some small edits (my grandma was not great with spelling), and a glossary to explain some of the terms that readers may not be familiar with. I hope you find it as charming as I do.

— Anastasia Rose

1952

Dear Diary,

It seems so good to have you to be my friend and record all my doings and troubles to you. You will soon know all of my secrets, and I hope you will be a true friend. I don't know why they named me Cathy, but I quite like it, although I am the only one in the family (of 10) with just one name.

I think I am awful tall, but some don't think so. I am 5 feet 5 ½ inches and will be 14 on Jan. 20th, just this month. Fourteen seems so old, quite grown up, but by the time I am about 19, when this diary will be complete, I'll think I was still quite a little girl at 14, probably. I have brown hair, not very long, and what most people say "pretty big blue eyes." Well, I guess I'm ok, but I hope I'm not conceited.

I like to do so many things. I don't quite know how to begin. First, I love to sing. I haven't had any training, but I hope I can go to college and really learn, or try to learn, how to sing good. I hope so, I like singing so well. Meanwhile, I will try to take every opportunity to sing I get.

About the 19th, I think I will sing in the 8th grade assembly. I hope – hope I can really put it over with everything I have got. I'll tell you the results. I believe I'll sing "When Irish Eyes Are Smiling."

I like to draw too. When I was 12, I think it was, I entered one of these "draw me's," or draw the girl and try for a lot of money or prizes. I just decided I would try it. The company wrote back and said I had talent and should enroll in their art school when I am 14. I should try again, to enter one of the contests later, and keep up my drawing. I'd like to go to college and take a class in art if I can. I like little kids and like to teach or tell them stories and things. I'd like to be a teacher. Mama wanted to be a teacher too, but she got married and didn't stay at college enough. I like to write and tell stories too.

I have always wanted to play a violin so much, but it has been out of the question. Now a good one is hard to find and costs so much. I always wished some ancestor would leave one for me, or I'd inherit one. Then I wanted a piano so it could help me learn to sing. Mama and Wendy always wanted one too. I don't know if you would call it inherited or not, but Uncle Logan and Aunt Natalie have a piano and Veronica doesn't want to play it, because it is all out of tune, and she didn't have any interest in it. So they said we could have it. Boy, weren't we thrilled! Then Roy didn't want it out of the family, I guess, and he wanted it when he gets married, so we get to learn on it and get it tuned, sort of for rent. I sure mean to learn how to play it. So does Wendy (she's my older sister by one year), and I sure appreciate her.

Seems so good to have a sister just older than you to give you advice and help – 'cept when you get the same boyfriend, ha, ha! I don't really mean it, but it's funny we both like Nathan Roberts ("The Bet"). Only it didn't make me and Wendy dislike each other, I hope! I don't know if he likes me or not. Sometimes I think he does, and sometimes I don't know. Wendy says she will give him up because she says she doesn't like him like I do. I'll never get to my history and tell you about myself if I get off on that.

Well about the first I remember, we have had the ranch. Golly! The dear old ranch, we love it so much. And now we won't live out there in the pretty green valley anymore, though we are not going to sell it. I hope. It was our 7th heaven out to "Hog's Heaven" named for Adam Jones, who homesteaded our lower meadow and was called a hog because the people around there wanted more land out there. Jones called them hogs, so they turned around and called him Hog Adam. I think it was mean.

I have always liked him, though I don't know him since he died about 45 – 50 years ago. It hasn't ever haunted me when they would say every moonlit night he would scarf dance on the golden stairs (a hill leading into Hog's Heaven), and he was buried at our lower meadow. I used to ask where, and they would say about over in the middle.

I have only been out there once, last summer (it's 40 miles out there), but Lincoln (age 16) and Ikie (age 10), my older brother and younger brother, said they (his folks) have done justice to the old man and placed a head stone at his grave and his little daughter's by him. I hope they rest in peace out there in the quiet where a car seldom comes, and there is nothing to disturb nature's quiet peace. When we moved in from there, we moved up above Glendale or North Glendale. We had a winter home at Orderville but sold it.

I better say good night now. I have got to help get my little brothers to bed.

January 1st, 1952 - Dear Diary, being the New Year, I get to write in you. For a long time, I have wished I had you, and this Christmas you were given to me. I hope we will be good friends.

New Year Resolutions:
  1. *Be quiet when I should be quiet (especially when Sammy is around)*
  2. *Have more patience with my brothers*
  3. *Not let little things get me down*
  4. *Keep my trouble (and thoughts) to myself*
  5. *Stop saying my thoughts*

6. *Watch 4 S's*
7. *Be happy and fun*

These are my New Year's resolutions. Number one means... well, I'll start from the first.

I like Nathan Roberts. I couldn't exactly say why. Then one dance night he danced with me, and his sister Jenny said she was pretty sure he liked me. Golly, you can't imagine how that affected me. I was so happy and excited. I just beamed and acted so funny everybody wondered what was the matter. The only trouble was Wendy likes him too. Heck, what should I do? It was that day, before the dance, she said she bet he danced with me, and probably before her. That was how he got the name "The Bet."

He did dance with me, and he didn't dance with her, so Wendy said, "I won't like him (like that) anymore." I guess it wasn't quite so hard for her to say she didn't like him anymore. I couldn't have ever said that though.

That night I had a new rival. Amy liked him too and asked him to let her sit by him on the bus – of course he had to say he would. When Amy got off from the bus for her stop, he asked me if I would play tic tack toe # on the frosty window. I said I would, so he reached over (he was sitting in the seat just back of me) and we played # on the window. Then he said to come back to his seat 'cause there was some more frost on that window, so I did. In a minute I was home, so he told me goodbye, and I got off the bus. Wendy said I was just beaming. Well, I just couldn't sleep that night.

Monday things went normal, but Nathan started to sit by Amy. What I was going to do was I would go to Wendy with all these troubles and thoughts and not let these little things get me down.

Things are going about the same, only Nathan doesn't sit by Amy so much and sometimes acts about like he might like me – just might. I'm not sure, so I won't chase him, just wait and see what happens. I'll let you know.

Oh! But I must tell you where #1 comes in. Here I was talking my thoughts again – and talking when I shouldn't have been – to LeAnn, my first cousin. I said, "Doesn't it make you feel good when you like somebody and you think maybe they like you?" I told her how I couldn't sleep that night, and of course Sammy heard, and of course there's nobody like Sammy (younger brother) for telling. He told Daddy, Uncle Logan, Uncle Lawrence, Roy, and even Amy that I told LeAnn this lingo.

Oh! But he makes me mad – so do I. If I could shut up when I should shut up, how better off I'd be.

Again, if anything happens I'll let you know (Golly, if somebody read this paper, wouldn't I get in a fix!).

January 2nd, 1952 - Well Dear Diary, school started today and so back in the old routine again with more assignments and work, but I kind of like school anyway. I have to ride the bus with my sister and four brothers.

January 3rd, 1952 - Dear Diary, it has been another school day. We had a pep assembly for the boys who are going down to play basketball with Dixie tonight. I hope they win.

January 4th, 1952 - Dear Diary, the boys were beat. I guess the Dixie team is one of the best teams in these parts. We have started the lead games with a loss, but I hope the boys will win most of them.

January 5th, 1952 - Dear Diary, today is Saturday, so I didn't go to school. Wendy and I have new curtains for our room and gave our old ones to the boys.

January 6th, 1952 - Dear Diary, today being Sunday, I went to Orderville to church. My cousin LeAnn, age 12, invited me to stay down to her house and have a candy pull with some other girls. It was fun.

January 7th, 1952 - Dear Diary, LeAnn, Chad (her brother), and I hurried to school this morning – but were told the furnace in the school building was broken. So we read, went sleigh riding, and had a good time in the snow.

January 8th, 1952 - Dear Diary, the furnace was soon fixed so we had school today, and I came home. I had been gone for about 2 days because I had no way home.

January 9th, 1952 - Dear Diary, in school today we had a band concert (I wish I could be in band), and the whole school had tests.

Dear Diary, Nathan doesn't seem to like anyone especially. He brings his harmonica and plays it on the bus. He sure can do it good. Sometimes I think it is for me. I hope Amy likes Leland (so does Wendy, a little) now, so she is about out.

Jenny wanted a picture of me, so she took one from my wallet. I said she could have it if she would trade it back for a better one of me when I got one, because it was awful.

This morning, she said Nathan took it (I wish I could get one of him). I'll think of a plan.

There will be a ballgame and dance Friday. I will tell you about it Friday night.

January 10th, 1952 - Dear Diary, the band took a concert over to Kanab today and that left only five girls and about nine boys in our class. Tomorrow night there will be a game and dance. Later, I will tell you about it.

January 11th, 1952 - Dear Diary, maybe it was just the dance or something, but I sure feel stupid, 'cause I am, I know. I will tell you all about it. Look at the paper.

Oh heck, Dear Diary, either me or somebody else is stupid, probably me.

I always have the worst luck. I started to get ready for the ballgame and dance. While Mama was trying to iron pleats in my last year's Christmas dress, she burned a hole in the bottom of it, so we had to cut it off even and hem it. It would take too long, so I wore the dress I wore that night. It's an awful pretty light blue with a big sash. I like it and my new black shoes.

Wendy fixed my hair a new way. Finally, it was time to go, and as we got on the bus I saw Nathan was there – really dressed up and his hair waved and combed so pretty (it's auburn, and I believe a little bit naturally curly). His eyes are the biggest and prettiest brown (Roberts brown). He was sitting alone. I sat just across from him. Arlene (a friend) came and sat by me. She likes Jim Martin. He sat by Nathan.

The game was pretty good, but Hurricane beat us quite a ways.

Before it started, Jenny and I went to call for the kids (Rose, Rita, Madeline). We were walking along and talking about Nathan. "I know he likes you, and the other day he said he likes Amy, but doesn't like her as much as he used to, but" – right then we saw a friend, and she walked on with us, so I don't know what she was going to say, and I guess I never will, but I believe it was something to follow. I know he likes you, but – but what?

After the game was over we, all the girls, went over to comb our hair and get ready for the dance. Soon it started, and as I am not so popular, I sat on the bench (with others). Nathan wasn't dancing either. Finally, as people were changing partners, I happened to glance up and saw Nathan. Something gave me the funniest feeling, even different from getting those excited butterflies in your stomach.

I didn't expect him to dance with me right off. He usually doesn't. And he didn't tonight either, he danced with his sisters, Byrdie, Jenny, and some of the kids his age (and friends).

Time wore on. Lincoln and a few other kids danced with me. But Nathan wouldn't. I wonder why? The dance would be out in a while, and I got to feeling low. Pretty soon, he tapped Rose on the shoulder and asked her for a dance, but I guess she had had it (quite popular), then he asked me. I don't know why, but I felt sort of second choice or something, but I smiled a little and went to dance with him.

He said something about the game. I said, "huh." I should have listened better, I guess. We talked a little, but I didn't do much of it. It was over in just a jiffy, and he said it sure was short. I agreed with him. He said thanks, and I said, "yah!" And I believe I gave his hand a squeeze. Then he had the funniest (surprised) expression. I don't know why, or if I should have done it. Then I danced with Lincoln. It's sure good to have a big brother.

I think for some reason I had made Nathan think I didn't like him or was bored or something, because I didn't act very glad to dance with him or talk much – but I do like him.

I asked Lincoln if he had liked a girl (maybe) and thought she liked him back, "would you dance with her?" He knew what I was trying to say and said I should act happier.

I noticed Nathan wasn't dancing any more, just sitting on the bench and looking sort of sad or something. Maybe he was just tired.

The dance ended, and Arlene and I hit out for the waiting bus. A few were already there, including Nathan. He was sitting alone about the fifth seat down.

All of the seats around him were taken, so I sat about the second seat down, and Rita Brown sat by me. Nathan was saving a place – he wouldn't let anybody sit by him, but a girl older than him sat by him anyway. He didn't want her to. Then this girl wanted to get closer to the front, so she asked Wendy to trade her places. She laughed it off and pointed to me. Fiona asked me. I didn't know if I should or not. Wendy said go ahead if you want to. So I did. I felt so silly. I sat on the edge of the seat and couldn't think of anything to say.

It was Arlene who told Fiona to have me come down. She was sitting on the seat just behind Nathan's with Jim. Nathan asked Jim to trade me places, then he called to Amy to trade me places. Oh imagine how I felt. Why, oh why, didn't he want me to sit by him? Amy came down and sat in-between us, and her and Nathan started to talk and laugh. Then at Wendy's motion, I moved and sat by Lincoln.

And Lincoln wondered what was the matter.

I got off the bus, and here I am.

I won't ever sleep tonight. Just worry and wonder what I should have done and what Nathan meant.

Goodnight.

January 12th, 1952- Dear Diary, today I have been brooding over boy troubles about (you know who), and I have been cleaning house. I sure don't feel well.

January 12th, 1952 - Dear Diary, it's me that's stupid. Mama said I probably hurt his feelings, and when I sat by him, I made him think I didn't enjoy it or want to. Oh, will I ever learn not to be so, oh so, stupid? I should have said, "Oh, I would like to sit by Nathan," and then do it happily and talk with him. He would probably beam, and everything would be okay.

If I could just not be so two S's - Serious and Silent - around him. I guess he thinks I'm stupid too. Another two S's - Stupid and Silly.

Another resolution should be watch those four S's.

And be happy, jolly, and forget this and have fun and be that way with him.

I wonder how this will ever turn out.

January 13th, 1952 - Dear Diary, it sure has been an awful Sunday for me. I have the sore throat, headache, and had to stay home all day.

January 14th, 1952 - Dear Diary, I stayed home from school today, because I still have a sore throat. Wendy has the measles, but she went to school today.

January 15th, 1952 - Dear Diary, it seems funny going to school today again. I am going to stay down at LeAnn's tonight (I think) for her birthday party (13th).

January 16th, 1952 - Dear Diary, last night I stayed at LeAnn's. I must practice right hard because our assembly is Friday.

January 17th, 1952 - Dear Diary, tomorrow is our assembly, and I am going to sing "When Irish Eyes are Smiling." Wish me luck.

January 18th, 1952 - Dear Diary, the bus slid off of the road at Alton so it didn't get to school until quite late. I sang my song and think I made a hit.

I haven't been to school since Friday. I wondered what Nathan would act like. This morning, I sat in the seat across from him.

Nothing ever happens in school, except when I meet him in the hall. I can't look at him and have to go up the hall for something I forgot (so does he). He plays (ping pong) in our first class in the morning before the bell rings.

I got on the bus and sat by another girl. The bus was about filled up when a group of boys (including Nathan) came in. Nathan stopped where I sat and stood for the longest time (probably waiting for the guy in front of him to move). Then, he went to the back of the bus.

When we reached the last stop in Glendale, the kids in the seat in front of me left. He came and sat there. He had some lipstick and raised his arm in the air and asked who wanted it. Quick for a chance, I said, "I do." He held it out to me, and I tried to take it but just pulled the top off. Then he smeared some on my hand. I tried to smear it back, but he said, "Don't get it on my coat." He asked for the lid back and said it was Joy's. He gave it to Becca. Soon we got home.

Dear Diary, today has been fine for me. You know how I love to sing. Well, I have been practicing ("When Irish Eyes are Smiling") to sing in our assembly. I knew I would be scared, but I wasn't very – and it was about like when I sang "Cruising Down the River" in the 5th grade. When I sang, I tried to do my best. I think I did do about my best too. Everybody liked it, and they clapped me out. Just think! I could do it over again and would like to. This morning, the bus didn't come until way after time because the bus slid off the road at Alton. In my hurry to get to the bus, I forgot the music to my song. But, luckily, Amy could play it by ear.

It was a different kind of school today having the assembly, and Mrs. Archer said she wouldn't come back to school again, and she hasn't yet. Mercy Cornellia has been taking her place. Then to make it worse, two of the teachers blamed three of the students for driving Mrs. Archer away, and they all felt bad and cried and said they wouldn't ever come back again. It was sure messed up. We had a pep assembly today too. The boys are going to Kanab, our neighboring town, to play basketball. Everybody yelled and are all in hopes we win the game. We just have to. I sure hope we can!!

School was let out at two because the electricity was off.

On the bus tonight – I will tell you what happened. Well, I will start with yesterday. Nathan seems to always sit back or right in front of me, but I doubt if he would sit by me. I was sitting on a seat to myself. Some boy came in and a boy, Bob (16), was just in front of Nathan.

He sat by me, and Nathan sat just behind me. Pretty soon, he gave my arm a knock with his (you see I had my arm on the back of the seat).

Of course I turned around. He winked at me. Of course I felt silly and probably showed it (don't think Nathan is that way, he just has fun and teases). I turned around, so he did it again. I tried to wink at him, but I didn't know how. He tried to show me how but couldn't. Then he took my arm and tried to put it around Bob. I wouldn't let him. And so there was quite a struggle.

"I wouldn't want to be your boyfriend, if you wouldn't even put your arm around me," he said.

Tonight, he sat just in front of me, and Wendy sat by me. She started to tease him by messing his hair up. Of course he enjoyed it and so did Wendy. I just sat there and burned. Wendy says she doesn't have my talents like I have. I told her, after Nathan moved up one and her over one, I said she had the talent of talking and having a good time and could win out that way. So she asked me to sing.

Bob was up farther in the bus, but I heard him ask who sang in our assembly or who I was. Then he asked where I was sitting. A boy in the seat in back of him put his hands over Bob's eyes. He wanted to know if it was me. Everybody roared – and Nathan tried, but wore the queerest expression.

Everybody wanted me to sing, so I did, but I couldn't get the right pitch to "When Irish Eyes are Smiling." A few of the kids hummed a few pitches (excluding Nathan). I sang quite a few songs then Wendy asked me to sing "Ramona," but some other girls said "Red Wing." Nathan wanted that too, so I sang it. As I got off the bus, I looked up and saw Nathan looking out the window. I smiled, but I don't think he saw it.

January 19th, 1952 - Dear Diary, today is Saturday – the day before my birthday. I have been cleaning house.

Tomorrow I will be fourteen (14). I hope it will be a good year. I have looked forward to it for so long.

January 20th, 1952 - Dear Diary, I must wish myself a happy birthday. I hope the year is to be a good one, my 14th. I went to church this morning and had a good Sunday.

January 21st, 1952 - Dear Diary, back to school again. We are sure having troubles. The teachers are against the students and the students against the teachers.

January 22nd, 1952 - Dear Diary, school is still the same mix up, and everybody doesn't know what to do – if they should go to a different school or kick the teachers out. I hope things turn out o.k.

Dear Diary, I am to school again, but Nathan hasn't been to school this week. Finally, I asked Jenny why. She said he fell off the horse and must have sprained a ligament in his leg because he can't hardly walk, and besides he had a cold. Poor guy, I hope he soon gets better.

After school, I was with Jenny waiting for the bus when Sammy called, "Hello Nathan" and kept calling me Nathan and saying everything he knew. He embarrassed me, and when I let on, he did it all the more. Then I saw somebody had written "Cathy & Nathan" on the wall. I'm just kind of glad Nathan wasn't around or there would be two of us embarrassed.

The shell pin I was wearing fell off, and somebody stepped on it and bended it. When I was trying to fix it, the bus came. So I got on and tried to fix it. Wendy tried to fix it, but she broke it. I felt awful. It was my best and only pin Daddy had given me.

Gwenda asked me to sing, but I told her I didn't feel like it.

Delbert said I wasn't all here, and Bob said, when Gwenda asked me to sing, "Oh that little Cornellia girl, where is she?"

Karan said, "Bob wants you to sing, and he likes you, so sing." But I wouldn't, because I didn't feel like it.

Today is Friday. I didn't think Nathan would come 'til Monday.

As I got on the bus, I saw the top of his head and knew it was him. I sat down as fast as I could and where I could (because I suddenly felt funny), by Jenny. She looked at me kind of funny. Maybe she saw I looked funny. The girls wanted me to sing. I felt happy and good, so I sang, but it was... it was rather weak and not very loud.

Nathan just acted kind of nothing out of the way. All day he acted sort of (Oh, not especially like me). Then on the bus, he sat by Wendy. They could always have a good time, and they did. Amy was sitting just in front of them. She was beaming too. Of course I was at the other end of the bus and was having a bad time. Bob doesn't seem to like me either. Eva let him take my mirror and use it. I wish Nathan could see.

There is a dance Saturday. I don't know if I want to go or not. The Alton orchestra is going to play, and you know what that means. Wendy is dancing in the floor show with a very pretty dress, and I am afraid what might happen.

But I am going to face it and whatever happens. I am not going to let it get me down. I will report.

It sure was a dumb dance. I didn't dance once, except with Lincoln, and Nathan didn't either, so I didn't feel so bad. Though Amy and Wendy were there. He just stood by the piano and his Dad's orchestra. Maybe his leg hurt.

January 23rd, 1952 - Dear Diary, nothing much ever happens. This week is just dragging, though I believe things are settling down.

January 24th, 1952 - Dear Diary, yesterday we had a 4-H exchange meeting. Today is another dull day for me.

January 25th, 1952 - Dear Diary, for some reason I wish school was just starting for the week. But I am afraid what might happen.

January 26th, 1952 - Dear Diary, tonight was the Gold and Green ball, but it wasn't a very good dance for me.

January 27th, 1952 - Dear Diary, today is Sunday. I went to Sunday school and meeting. They sure were good (I mean meeting). It was about tolerance.

January 28th, 1952 - Dear Diary, it is Monday today. We are having a party and inviting Logan and Natalie down for home evening.

Dear Diary, today was Monday. The day went o.k. but Wendy sure likes Nathan and shows it. I am afraid he likes her, and I don't know what to do. I am so very different from Wendy, and she knows just how to act. She says to remember she likes him too, maybe even as much as I do, but I don't see how she could. His name is Karl Nathan.

January 29th, 1952 - Dear Diary, tonight was Mutual, and it was a very good one. I must remember it.

I guess it's, "Oh jealous heart, stop your pounding," for me. I don't know why, but even if he looks at Wendy or anything like that, I just burn. I know I shouldn't, but it makes me feel so awful towards Wendy or whom it may concern. Why am I this way? Tonight he sat across from her and looked so serious and (that look), it makes me feel so awful, and it shouldn't.

Tonight was Mutual, and Roy took us as usual. We had such a good class, you know the kind that makes you want to be better, and find how you can, and how bad you really are. I read the story of Joseph Smith and thought how jealous I was and knew I shouldn't. But how could I get so it wouldn't make me feel that way?

Going home, Roy said (he had said before) to tell him our problems and maybe he could help.

So I asked him how I could get over being so – jealous of such little things, and we talked everything over. It really helped me. Wendy said she was not chasing Nathan or anything – so I just felt better.

I must remember these things:
1. *Not take things so serious.*
2. *Things aren't as bad as they seem, it is just how you look at them.*
3. *Never plan and scheme ahead for things to happen.*
4. *Be your own self.*
5. *Try to look and act happy.*
6. *Don't let little things you shouldn't worry about get you down.*

January 30th, 1952 - Dear Diary, today it seems like spring. The snow is melting, and the sun shines, and everything seems so good, only I have a cold.

Dear Diary, I believe a good share of the things I thought may not even be true.

February 29th, 1952 - Say, old "Dear Diary," stop locking on me! I haven't been able to write because your lock stuck (have I been mistreating you?).

March 1st, 1952 - The people we must associate with may be good and bad, but the bad seem to outcry the good, so we only hear them. Let's don't rush out into the streets to join them.

March 2nd, 1952 - Dear Diary – just haven't written to you for so long – nothing much has happened, so you didn't miss much. Today was a good day for me. I went to three meetings.

March 3rd, 1952 - Dear Diary, I went to a Dixie College band concert today. It was ever so nice, and I finally got enough courage to ask Mr. Williams if I might sing in the solo-ensemble, but he discouraged me. It is for good singers and high schoolers.

March 4th, 1952 - Dear Diary, today we were to see a puppet show but got word we couldn't, so today was another Tuesday. I went to Mutual, and we had a good class.

Dear Diary, things have their ups and downs, if you know what I mean. That's the way things are going now.

March 5th, 1952 - Dear Diary, all of the school got to go to a meeting today except 7th and 8th grades. Jenny stayed with me until her folks came and got her because we got left from the bus.

Jenny and I got left from the bus tonight. We started to walk home, and Roy picked us up and phoned Jenny's folks (thank goodness for.Roy). She said Nathan asked his dad if he could take the car. I asked, "What for?" Nathan said, "Oh, I would go down and get Amy." (He was just teasing, Jenny said, but you can't ever tell). Then she said that Nathan said Amy had a good personality and was cute, but Cathy is – I got the impression that she meant "diviner still," get it? I didn't hardly catch it. Jenny found out a lot and said she wouldn't tell anything, but I don't know. Nathan acted rather funny today. Although he didn't sit by Amy.

March 6th, 1952 - Dear Diary, today was Mary Ann's birthday. She was one, and Mama made a cake for her.

March 7th, 1952 - Dear Diary, the 8th grade boys played basketball with the 9th grade boys. We won by one point, but some say Mr. Luke was too much on our side. Mr. Bommis showed us slides on Germany.

March 8th, 1952 - Dear Diary, today was the usual Saturday, but today I entered a "draw me" or drawing a girl for a prize.

March 9th, 1952 - Dear Diary, I went to church today (meeting and Sunday school) and this evening tended the kids upstairs, while the folks had study club.

March 10th, 1952 - Dear Diary, it has been snowing all day today, and the snow is really piling up. I guess we won't have spring for a while.

March 10th, 1952 - Dear Diary, in my talks with Mama—well see I don't know how to act around most, some people (you can guess)—she says to smile more and you know some of those "little things." She said I take him wrong (all his acts).

March 11th, 1952 - Dear Diary, today it has been snowing, and tonight it was so very pretty when we came home from M.I.A., and we had one of our discussions.

March 12th, 1952 - Dear Diary, it was Rita's birthday today so she invited me to stay down and go to the party. I sure had fun.

March 13th, 1952 - Dear Diary, today has been fine but snow keeps coming. Jay came up and talked to us this evening.

March 14th, 1952 - Dear Diary, tonight I went to the "Junior Jump." After a hard time getting down, the bus didn't run. It wasn't too good of a dance.

March 15th, 1952 - Dear Diary, I have been home all day doing house work. Lincoln went to Kanab and got a pattern for me for a new dress.

March 16th, 1952 - Dear Diary, today was a good Sunday – but I didn't go to meeting.

March 19th, 1952 - Today, Dear Diary, I rode down to Mt. Carmel tonight – everyone got on the bus at our stop but nobody sat by me. Then Nathan passed by and said to Jenny, who was sitting just in back of me so I could hear, "I'd sit by Cathy if I thought she liked me." Then he sat by her. I turned around, and I asked, "Who said I didn't like him?" He said my little brother. We made a bet on it (a nickel). They really talk – Sammy and Ikie.

March 21st, 1952 - Dear Diary, there was a dance (Senior Hop). It was decorated very pretty and was fun, although the bus didn't run.

March 22nd, 1952 - Dear Diary, I stayed home all day today. It looks like it might be spring.

March 23rd, 1952 - Dear Diary, I went to all of the meetings. Mr. Williams and Mrs. Sorensen talked in meeting on good subjects.

Dear Diary, maybe I could learn to dance if I had a little more confidence in myself. Mama says I want to too much. It is like trying to catch a ball. If you tensely reach for it, it stings your hands. But if you let it come easily to you, you can catch the ball. I am a lot that way with things. I meet things half way instead of letting them come to me.

If I know all about it, why can't I do it?

March 24th, 1952 - Dear Diary, today they had an assembly for the ones going to the Spring Festival. I wish I was going.

March 25th, 1952 - Dear Diary, it is surely getting spring. I sure get lonesome for summer. Today was a good day.

March 26th, 1952 - Dear Diary, tonight we had a party at Aunt Arvilla's. Fred is home now.

March 27th, 1952 - Dear Diary, it has been a good school day today, and tonight I saw the play "Petticoat Ranch."

March 28th, 1952 - Dear Diary, today was the time we were to have our class dance, but we have cancelled it. We all (the school) danced today (together).

March 29th, 1952 - Dear Diary, today was Saturday. I worked cleaning the house and the yards.

March 30th, 1952 - Dear Diary, we had Sunday school and meeting at night. Oh, they were good. I went on the hill today for the first time since fall.

March 31st, 1952 - Dear Diary, I feel extra good now days – maybe it's spring fever. But I still wish I could understand myself along with a few others.

April 1st, 1952 - Dear Diary, we are going to have our dance on May 9th. Tonight we had an M.I.A. backwards dance and party.

April 2nd, 1952 - Dear Diary, the bank slid in and blocked the highway, so the road was closed, and we had to walk home.
    You know, I believe I am smarter than I use to be, but I still act rather silly. Let me tell you what happened today. It is April Fools, and we have sure had a fooling on the dates of our dance. Then to make things even worse, Arlene, who is a lot ornerier than she used to be, said, "I bet you wouldn't like Nathan if you heard him say what I did." She said it was bad. All I could find

out was that he thought I looked like a pig, had a nose as long as a blade of grass, and he didn't like me.

You can guess how that made me feel! He does kind of look like a donkey. I erased his name off my book. When everyone (Glendale) got off, Nathan moved into the seat just in front of me. He had glasses on upside down. He did look like a donkey. He moved his glasses back and forth at some kids and asked them if they liked him. Rita told him to ask me. He did, but like a dope I couldn't say anything, just smiled and went red. So he thinks I don't.

Roy says to ask him to the girls' day dance the 11th of April. I'd like to, but do you think I would dare?

April 3rd, 1952 - Dear Diary, Lincoln went to Salt Lake today and will be back Sunday. It was a Seminary trip to Conference.

April 4th, 1952 - Dear Diary, I stayed down to LeAnn's for Madeline's party. I had a lot of fun. It is Roger's birthday too.

April 5th, 1952 - Dear Diary, I came home early this morning and got my work done, then us kids went to the show "Sampson and Delilah."

April 6th, 1952 - Dear Diary, I went to church as usual today. There were not many there because of conferences. The school teachers talked.

April 7th, 1952 - Dear Diary, we had school for only half a day. We were let out for Arbor Day to clean up our yards.

Oh Dear Diary, I wish I could, but how on earth can I? I haven't a car and neither has he. Rita says to ask somebody in Glendale instead, and we could get her Dad to get him, but I just can't. Either I ask Nathan or not anybody.

April 8th, 1952 - Dear Diary, today in school there was a basketball game between the Juniors and Sophomores. The Juniors were beat.

Oh Dear, the time is getting closer and closer to the 11th. I just found out the bus won't run. What will I do? Hope I don't have to give up. Wendy and Lincoln both have dates.

April 9th, 1952 - Dear Diary, the 11th is girls' day – and a dance that night – here's hoping – I'll have to use my courage.

If there is a will, there's a way. Guess what! Roy (the angel) came down tonight and said he could take me and Nathan (Golly!!). I'm sure glad. But dare I ask him? Here's my plan.

Tomorrow morning when I get on the bus I will find a way to sit by him or close to him anyway. Wendy says she let on that I might ask him, so he will be expecting it. See you tomorrow. Wow – I'm excited!!

April 10th, 1952 - Dear Diary, criminy, oh I feel awful, sort of like laughing and sort of like crying (what a queer feeling!), and the weather really fits my mood, a dark raining storm that won't hardly break, black and dismal.

This morning, when I finally got on the bus after trying to eat breakfast, I found Roger had beaten me to it. He was sitting by him so I didn't have a chance to ask him then. So (I have been noticing lately we must pass the same part of the hall for second class), I hurried and took my book (History) in the room and made my way back to my locker to pretend I had forgotten my pencil.

There was hardly anyone in the hall, and who should be walking past but he himself in his new blue F.F.A. coat and all. I hurried up to him and (it must have been to stop him) put my hand on his arm and smiled a little and felt myself go red and saw him go red.

Well, I asked him. I don't really know what I said, but I had done it. Still smiling he said, "I haven't any way." And I said, "I have." "Well I'll think about it," he said. And he went into English. He was still smiling but still, maybe he didn't really want to go. But I'd find out. All day I tried to get a chance to ask him if he had "thought yet." Then school was out. Everything was gloomy and a storm was gathering. It made me feel dreary myself. I waited and waited and finally the bus came. I sat by Rose Mary. I saw Nathan get on and walk down the aisle and, oh Dear Diary imagine, sit by Amy.

Something and every feeling I ever had for either one of them, especially Nathan, turned the other way. I just sat there and stared out of the window – I have never felt so horrible in all my life. I swear I hated him with all my might. Wendy tapped me on the shoulder and said, "Have you asked him if he had thought yet or are you going to?"

"I don't know," I said. But it was hard because something was caught in my throat.

If anybody was mad it was Wendy, and she said "Don't."

What on earth was he trying to do? What on earth?

I know everybody could tell how I felt, but I didn't care.

Then Ikie started to tease, and oh what misery. I looked back at Nathan, and he was having a good time talking and was laughing at Amy.

Steven said something about Ted, and I tried to smile at him – but I didn't know what he meant. I understand Amy had asked Ted. I didn't care either way.

Glendale got off, and Wendy started to talk to me so Nathan could be sure and hear. I believe she said something about "tell her yourself." Nathan started to say, "Cathy, Cathy." I didn't look around until he said it quite a few times. It seems he said it sort of sorry and desperate like. "I'll give you my answer in the morning," he said. I smiled weakly and said, "OK," and got off the bus. Then is when I got that funny feeling. It all seemed so funny and when I would laugh I would just about cry and would have to stop. Then I would start to get shaky, and I don't know what all. I wanted to laugh so bad – but I couldn't.

I got the advice to ask Steven if Nathan didn't give me his answer in the morning, see because maybe he didn't want to go with me and that was his excuse, and to show Nathan I had a little spunk. Roy came down and asked if I had my date, and I told him I would know in the morning.

I really wonder what Nathan was trying to do. See if he could get Amy to ask him too? Trying to see what I would do? Didn't realize what he was doing? But then what was he doing just sitting by Amy? Ikie and Amy were playing horse shoes with Nathan and were following him around and what was she trying to do? She had already asked Ted. Criminy! I can't help it. If Nathan likes Amy because she can laugh, talk, and have a good time when she's with him, who wouldn't like her? But I am not Amy, and I won't be her. So see I am just naturally out. But he did say he would give me his answer. So I can look forward to that, and I could ask Steven if Nathan doesn't want to. It's funny. I can talk and have a good time with Steven, but he is shorter than me and is just a little boy, but he's fun.

April 11th, 1952 - Dear Diary, girls' day was really a big affair. We girls had assemblies, a tea, and only two classes. For the dance, see notes:

Dear Diary, today has been a great big day. I will begin at this morning. I got on the bus not knowing what to expect and found a seat close to the front and didn't turn around and tried to look happy. Nathan wasn't anywhere on the bus and I didn't know what to think. Soon, we came to Steven's stop, and I watched everyone get on the bus, but no Steven. Guess how I felt! Everything sank.

I walked to school not knowing what to do. Then Amy started to saying how she had asked Ted not Nathan, and I felt like saying, "You can have them both." Suddenly, Steven popped up from nowhere, and I felt more hopeful.

It seemed Jenny acted awful strange. Maybe she was afraid I would ask or say something, so I wrote a note to her like this:

Dear Jenny,

What's the matter with Nathan? Why didn't he come to school today — or isn't it any of my business? Did he tell you to tell me anything? Just answer yes or no.
C.C.

See I have to know what to plan for.
She wrote this back:

The horse bucked him off, and he hurt his ankle. No, he didn't tell me to tell you anything.
Jenny

Doesn't that sound kind of fishy like? Funny why it happened at such a time. Maybe it was just a coincidence. He just might have hurt it on purpose or told a little white lie. On the other hand, you just can't tell.

Well to make a long story short, I asked Steven to go with me, and Rita asked Errol. We took them in Roy's car. Roy and Allison and Lincoln and Annie.

Oh it was fun, and a little bit funny. Like when we went to get Steven, he came running out just as we stopped, and I got out to direct him where to go and got muddy.

Next, his corsage wouldn't stay on, and we lost the pin. I danced and danced until my feet ached and really enjoyed myself, and showed Jenny and Becca I was. They both came. It would be lovely if Nathan would have come marching in, wouldn't it!

Another funny thing was when we let Steven off. Like Rita did, I was going to go with him to the door, but he climbed out and shut the door. Meanwhile I was getting out, so I got bumped on the head. He said, "Oh, I'm sorry." And I said, opening the door wider, "Well goodnight, and thanks."

It really was fun anyway.

I can hardly wait (or can I?) till Monday to see how things will go.

I will let you know.

April 12th, 1952 - Dear Diary, I went to Kanab today and found out I am to wear glasses. Oh dear. And I saw a very good show, "From Real Big Places."

April 13th, 1952 - Dear Diary, today is Easter, so we tried to make it an extra good Sunday to remember what Jesus has done for us.

April 14th, 1952 – Monday—Nothing happened, and I don't think it will.

April 16th, 1952 - They've been practicing for "Saucy Hollindaze," an opera for the 23rd.

April 18th, 1952 – Friday—Still nothing. Nathan is to school without even a limp, but he told Lincoln his leg was sore (isn't he ornery?).

April 20th, 1952 - Dear Diary, do you think I ought to improve my handwriting? If I don't, I don't see how you will be able to read it.

April 21st, 1952 - Funny, but I believe it's true, that the way you feel will affect the way you write.

April 23rd, 1952 - Dear Diary, I went to the opera tonight. It was very good, with (guess who?) as main (Singing Prince) actor.
    Kind of blowing over (passing storm).
    Dear Diary, nice to have a wind to help the storms blow over. It seems like nothing ever happened.
    Only listen—I have something nice to tell you.
    Tonight was the opera, and Nathan took the main part (the prince). It was very good, and my! Can't somebody sing! I will always remember when "What is Love" was sang in a clear rich tenor by someone dressed in a blue uniform with golden braid.
    Once, I happened to glance his way, and what a smile was given me.

My!! Do I sound silly? I really am not boy crazy, it is just how I feel. Oh, I would like to be in an opera. I just long to sing. Maybe someday I will have the chance. Maybe next year. I'll be in high school then. I like to draw too. This summer I am going to draw lots, if I get a chance. And me and Wendy will put on operas. It sounds silly, but it's fun.

I get so darn lonesome for summer and old Hog's Heaven. But it's "Just a Memory." We used to go out at night when the moon was full and bright and put on plays and sleep out on the lawn. This summer, I hope I can go out for a while.

April 24th, 1952 - Dear Diary, there aren't many things going on this week, so I haven't written. But it is the day before the prom today, and you will never guess what happened!

My Dearest Diary, criminy!! I'll give you three guesses. What do you think just happened? Oh, I am so thrilled, imagine. Oh Dear Diary – It's hard to tell. It all went like this:

Lincoln is to take Annette to the dance tomorrow, some proposition with Roy. This morning, as I was going down the hall to Seminary, I saw Nathan talking with Annette at the other end of the hall. He happened to see me and turned on one foot towards me, then back around. I got the funniest darn feeling, and I had it all during Seminary. After Seminary, Jenny and I walked up to the building together.

As we entered the hall, Nathan was at the corner by the fountain. He had Jenny's lunch ticket for her, and I turned the corner and started up the hall. He stopped me, "Wendy wanted me to give you your ticket." I smiled and took it. "Now just one little question, will you go to the prom with me?"

I am still in a daze! But he said it. I can still hear and see just the way he looked and said it. I don't know exactly what I said, but it was something like, "Oh yes, sure!!" I didn't know what to do. I suddenly lost my appetite and knew I couldn't eat. I stumbled into the dressing room all a beam and in smiles. Jenny said, "You didn't think he liked you, did you? That shows you." She said it to tease me. I didn't eat much lunch, and I swear I could smell blossoms.

April 25th, 1952 - Dear Diary, today has been the most glorious day. Guess what! I just went to the dance with Nathan Roberts.

April 26th, 1952 - Dear Diary, I went to St. George today to be baptized, 10 times, for the dead. We made a day of it, and oh what fun.

What a night it was, Dear Diary. Nathan sat by me on the bus, and as quick as I got home I started getting ready. I had the prettiest "pink" dress, organdy with a blue ribbon. It seemed like all the while I was in a trance. Wendy and Lincoln went with Roy to Alton to get Annette and Nathan. I got all ready and was so excited and kind of nervous. I was in the living room, just fixing my hair, when I heard voices and the door open.

They were here. Nathan came in and stood by the door (and crossed his legs in that cute way of his). I knew I went red, and I couldn't think of what to do. Daddy and all of the kids were there, and I thought Daddy was going to laugh or the boys would say something. I went closer to the door, and Nathan said, "Here's your corsage, but it's just a homemade one." I smiled and said "All the better."

It was wrapped in wax paper and joined with a straight pin. It seemed like my hands went shaky, but I got it unwrapped, and oh Dear Diary, gosh it was pretty (I can look over on the shelf and still see it)! It's two pink roses in the center with two yellow buds and another pink one surrounded by green leaves and set on a wide, light blue ribbon. It will never wilt because it was something better than just flowers, it was made of pretty organdy just like my dress, and it was the perfect match for it. Wendy helped me pin it on.

Mama told Nathan to sit down (I had not told him). He sat down on the couch by Roger. He told us our dresses were pretty. I wanted Wendy to pin a ribbon on hers, and Nathan told her too, so it would be like mine, so she did. We went out to the car, and

Nathan opened the back door for me, and I slid in by Annette. Then he got in.

At the dance, we walked in together. He paid our tickets. We walked through the green hallway, and he helped me take off my coat. We went in and started to dance. It sure was decorated pretty, with 6 rose covered pillars, a branch of a blossomed tree beside a bench, and a little bridge in the end of the gym. The ceiling and walls were decorated with two shades of green and trellises of flowers. The orchestra (Sky Lighters) were in one corner.

We danced two dances, then I sat down and saw the other girls. Amy was there and was doing a good job of acting not jealous. I had a good time. But I felt so funny, just like as if everything was a dream and not real at all. (I will always remember it, I can't forget it). I didn't know when the dance would be over and was surprised when I was dancing with Lincoln to hear it was the last dance. Then Nathan came for me and took my hand. Soon we had made our way out and found my coat.

Early the next morning, we girls were going to go to St. George to the temple to get baptized for the dead, and we were going to stay down at Rose's.

I didn't know how to tell him, but soon he said, "You're going to stay down to Rose's, aren't you?"

"Yes."

"Then I will take you down there." We walked down the path. His hand felt warm and good. Golly! I like him. He was saying something about his Dad being back from shearing, and we talked about that. "What if we beat Rose home?" he said.

"I think her mother will be there," I said. Then I got to thinking. I had seen her at the dance, so I told him.

"Should we go talk to Mama?" he said, or something like that, but I had already said, "Oh there's probably somebody home." It seems like I made quite a few little blunders like that. I hope he didn't take me wrong, because I would have liked to talk to his mother, but I had slipped in too many extra words. We walked on. (Oh, I hoped he liked me). I wondered if he did, and how much (wished I could tell). We watched the cars come racing down the road with all their lights shining and horns blowing. It was a sight. We waited by the corner for a minute then almost ran across the road and stopped at the other side.

"I wonder if anybody will be home." A passerby seeing Carl's café marveled to us how full it was. "He's got lots of business tonight."

Nathan said, "Should we go over there?" I hesitated a minute. "It's up to you," he said.

"Sure let's go." It was crowded, so we went into the dining room and found Rose, Madeline, and Verue with their dates there at a long table. Nathan sat a chair for me and found him one by me. He asked what I wanted and, like a dope, I hesitated again.

"Whatever you want," he said. Finally I said, "a malt." That was about all I knew how to say and could think of. "Chocolate." Nathan ordered the same. We had a race drinking it, and it was a tie. It seemed like Nathan was extra quiet. He was probably tired. He had said he was.

We watched Charles flip quarters and talked a little. We stayed for quite a while. We noticed Wendy, Roy, Lincoln, and Annette had come in the café. We left with the other kids. Funny, I didn't know if I should let him take my hand or how to let him. The other kids weren't far, so we walked a little way behind – and soon we were all in one crowd by Rose's porch. Seems like I couldn't find Nathan. Then I heard him say, "Good night," and I said, "Good night," and he was off to find Roy.

"Gosh, I had had fun and would always, always remember it." The lingering, somehow haunting, perfume of the pink roses and yellow buds. The swirl of my first pink dancing dress, the touch of a hand, the thrill and joy of it all, all entwined in a soft golden memory to hold dear, forever.

It was hard to sleep that night and all of us girls talked, laughed, and raced around until, imagine, 4:00 o'clock. We finally got to sleep and woke up to Gwenda's call at 6:00 o'clock to get ready to go to St. George at 7:00. Most of us girls rode down with Roy. We went to the temple at 9:00, and were baptized 10 times a piece. It was very pretty down there. Everything was green and in bloom. It rained a little, and the sun played about among the trees. Our temple stood solemn and white above it all, wrapped in its own holy silence.

At twelve, we had a lunch and visited the stores. Later we went in swimming. Then started on our way. We kids persuaded Roy into letting us go again into the hot springs, and I learned how to swim. That night, we went to the movie "Fancy Pants" at Orderville.

Tired but happy, I got home late and piled into bed. I had to keep pinching myself. Had all this really, honest to goodness, happened? Then I would look at my corsage—it must have!

April 27th, 1952 - Dear Diary, although I am tired, I went to church and have had a good day.

April 28th, 1952 - Dear Diary, nothing much has happened today. Only another sunny spring day, and the fruit trees are in bloom.

April 29th, 1952 - Dear Diary, I got my glasses today. We went to Mt. Carmel to dance for M.I.A.

April 30th, 1952 - Dear Diary, I act kind of silly, I guess, don't I?

May 1st, 1952 - Dear Diary, today I got the best complement and from all people, Mr. Williams. He said I could sing and had improved 200% since last year.

May 2nd, 1952 - Dear Diary, tonight was the post prom, but I didn't go, and I didn't even want to.

May 3rd, 1952 - Dear Diary, guess what? We got a new machine, just what we need., especially dear Mama. She really needs one.

May 4th, 1952 - Dear Diary, of all things a new lawn mower and new water, criminy! Things are really happening.

May 5th, 1952 - Dear Diary, I forgot to tell you yesterday, Melvin (our first cousin) and his new wife came to see us. We hadn't seen Melvin for about 8 or 10 years.

May 6th, 1952 - Dear Diary, it is spring! And everything is lovely, apple blossoms, and new leaves turning. The whole earth smells new and clean.

May 7th, 1952 - Dear Diary, things are the same as they ever were, but school is getting too tiresome, but soon it will be out. Guess what? I got all A's on my report card.

May 8th, 1952 - Dear Diary, tomorrow is going to be a big day and night too. V day and then our dance. I am going to stay at Rita's.

May 9th, 1952 - Dear Diary, V day today and our dance tonight. There wasn't many out, but then it turned out o.k., and Rita and I went home to bed on the back porch.

Well it's V day. Today we had a show, and my! Amy is trying hard to win some attention. That means more work for me.

May 10th, 1952 - Dear Diary, I came home at 10:00 and have been working all day – and from last night too – I sure am tired.

May 11th, 1952 - Ikie's birthday.

Dear Diary, today has been a big day for me. Best of all, the 8th grade graduated from Seminary. Oh, it was a fine program.

Today was a day to remember. We graduated from Jr. Seminary. I wore my pink dress and corsage, although Nathan wasn't there.

Hal Taylor talked and oh, it was good. He talked about on the right path and if we knew which way north is.

May 12th, 1952 - Dear Diary, I stayed home today so Mama and Roger could go to Panguatch. It is a pretty day and good to be alive.

Dear Diary, please don't get the wrong impression of me. I don't think of Nathan all the time. I live and look forward to other things, this is just my secret thoughts and affairs along that line. I have been accused of "thinking too much along that line," but I have higher aims.

May 13th, 1952 - Dear Diary, in M.I.A. we saw pictures on 4-H. They were very good. Then I went to Rita's while the others had dance practice.

My! Dear Diary, guess what I just heard?

Rita sat by LeAnn in church, and she heard a lot from LeAnn. "Nathan just hates Cathy," she said, "and Jenny said he likes me. The only reason he took her to the dance was because of that girls' day affair, and he thinks she is a boy chaser." (See Jenny stayed down to my place).

Criminy!! Isn't that nerve for you? Who does she think she is?

I am going to act better to Nathan and be more sociable (if I dare and can). He must think I am stuck up the way I act, but he just sort of scares me, and I just can't, although I doubt if what LeAnn said is true, and (I don't care) so there!

May 14th, 1952 - Dear Diary, today was the Sophomore assembly and the day to get more assignments. Early tomorrow the high school is going to Zion National Park. (I hope I have fun).

May 15th, 1952 - Dear Diary, sure I had fun. As fun as could be expected, but now I feel mighty tired. Seems like I am tired most of the time (school I guess).

Dear Diary, we went on our school trip today. It was sure fun, but now I have the worst feeling. On the bus, Nathan teased Amy and enjoyed himself. Naturally, I slunk back and tried not to watch (when I should have got in on it like Amy would have). But I didn't, and I won't, so ho, ho Nathan! You can't make me (probably that's what he was trying to do). He makes me mad, although he did let me in on it a little. I think he's ornery, and what's more, he ripped my hat Wendy was wearing.

For ornery, Dear Diary, listen to this.

Maybe it's his way or something, probably (something) but Nathan sure isn't very sociable. He has cut his hair in the new fashion (crew cut). Wish he wouldn't have, but it is his hair, not mine.

May 16th, 1952 - Dear Diary, it's funny, half of the kids who went on the trip didn't come back today. Wonder why? And guess what I heard?

Well Dear Diary, some folks are sure awful. You know LeAnn thinks she likes him, and my how she shows him. It's not just me who thinks she is a flirt either. She wants something, and she usually gets it.

Tonight she came to me and said, "Oh Cathy, I am awful sorry. Jenny says Nathan likes me," and she made over how she isn't chasing him, or liking him in anyway. "Oh, I am so sorry," she said!

"Well," I said, "I am not. I am glad he is liked." And so on, just showing her I didn't care (or trying to).

I am not as dumb as she thinks I am. She usually gets what she wants and has her own clever little schemes to do it. She is truly a flirt, and maybe I can't say any more for Nathan. He has her watch and yields to her little plans and is certainly fickle, or maybe he doesn't know what goes. How dumb is he? Or maybe it's me who's dumb? Criminy!!

My! My! What I didn't hear, Dear Diary.

I found out LeAnn was sitting in between Nathan and Errol on the way back home.

Don't be surprised at what might happen, the way Rita and I feel! Ever since last night, I felt wicked, so guess how I feel now? H-E-double toothpicks! The dear ornery little flirt, or should I say flirts.

Then LeAnn told Rita a lot and said Jenny told her. I sort of asked Jenny, and she said not to let anything LeAnn said worry me. I don't think Jenny would betray or tell on me, she just isn't that kind (I hope). LeAnn could have told some little white lies.

Doesn't it make you mad? First Ted, now Nathan and Errol. Rita feels mad about that too. Only Errol has a little bit of sense, I think, so maybe he will catch on. (She kisses Jenny and says it is for Nathan). For stupid.

May 17th, 1952 - Dear Diary, today I cleaned the front room and the milk house, then I studied my Science.

Dear Diary, I feel sorry for LeAnn, but even if I forgive her and things pass over, I will never feel for her like I use to. I just can't, neither will some other kids I know. And Dear Diary, do you really think I should blame Nathan for letting a girl sit by him and talk with him? I would let another boy (maybe), but maybe that's beside the point. (I just wonder what the future holds). Kind of dumb (all), isn't it?

May 18th, 1952 - Dear Diary, today after church company came, Chick and Jean and the family. My, it was good to see them. Then Daddy's cousins came.

Dear Diary, tonight at about 6:00, Wendy and I were sitting on the lawn, when down the highway came a white sheep wagon. Nathan was sitting out at the back. He was blatting as loud as he could and sounded like a sheep. I bet I won't see any more of him for a long time. He was going to the herd probably (maybe I won't even see him all summer).

May 19th, 1952 - Dear Diary, it's the last Monday of this school year. I am kind of glad – but I am getting lonesome for the ranch. It is the first summer in 10 or 11 years we haven't moved.

My mistake, he was to school today.

May 20th, 1952 - Dear Diary, tonight we went over to Kanab for the Spring Festival (M.I.A.). There was a big crowd and everybody was there (almost). I saw L. J. H.

And the same as ever, but every day he doesn't come to school on the bus, but with his Dad, then going home he rides to

Glendale then gets off on the first bus stop, then about 6:30 he comes home with his dad. (Maybe he works or something).

Just think, tomorrow is the last day of school and the last dance. (No more worries but, oh dear).

May 21st, 1952 - Dear Diary, today the Seniors had their assembly. It was so darn sad. We'll sure miss them next year, especially Louana and Delwin.

May 22nd, 1952 - Dear Diary, today was the last day of real school, and we played ball about half of the time. Just think, tomorrow is the last day of school.

May 23rd, 1952 - Dear Diary, another school year has passed. It seems like it went so fast. I guess it was a good year, but I will miss school. (Tonight was commencement dance).

May 24th, 1952 - Dear Diary, today I house cleaned, and they had our first 4-H meeting, but of course I couldn't go to it.

Dear Diary, well school is out, and I won't be seeing any of the kids and Nathan for a while. It was a good dance tonight, so was the graduation. Guess who wasn't there and hasn't been to school lately? Jim says he's shearing. Who cares? Do you? I shouldn't.

Here's saying good bye for that subject. Dismissed.

I've acted pretty dumb, come to think about it. Maybe I had better change my ideas and notions.

May 25th, 1952 - Dear Diary, today I met Marylou's husband (to be). He's nice.

May 26th, 1952 - Dear Diary, it seems kind of strange not going to school, and you get kind of restless, but I had a fine day, and I drew some pictures.

May 27th, 1952 - Dear Diary, I went to M.I.A. tonight and learned about flower arrangement. I'm about to get lonesome.

May 29th, 1952 - Oh, I'm lonesome.

May 30th, 1952 - I did my house work today, because tomorrow is swarm day at Zion.

May 31st, 1952 - Dear Diary, it was a grand day, and I stayed down at LeAnn's. I went to "The Painted Hills."

June 1st, 1952 - Dear Diary, I feel different about the church. I think it is true, but my faith is not near strong enough.

June 2nd, 1952 - I didn't do much today but remember how lonesome I am.

June 3rd, 1952 - Dear Diary, I went to town today to 4-H, and Rita asked me to stay down. Goody! And maybe I can (next week). A big day for Roy, his wedding.

June 4th, 1952 - Dear Diary, it was Daddy's birthday today, but he is out to the ranch. That's where he likes to be, and I can't blame him.

June 5th, 1952 - Dear Diary, I guess I am not so lonesome now. Wendy and I went on the hill today and had a good time, and I can wander most anytime.

June 6th, 1952 - Dear Diary, I'm still lonesome. I don't know what for. I've been reading a lot, but most of it makes it worse. Wendy says it is because we aren't really living. We used to at the ranch.

June 7th, 1952 - Dear Diary, I did my Saturday work today and went in swimming for the first time this summer. I am going to stay at Rita's.

June 8th, 1952 - Dear Diary, after church I went to Rita's. We caught up on my 4-H, and we tended her sister's girls, then slept out.

June 9th, 1952 - Dear Diary, today has been fun. Rita and I washed, and later we (kids) had a party on the hill with wieners and all.

June 10th, 1952 - Dear Diary, we tended kids again and went to M.I.A. We're (Mia Maids) now. I was supposed to go home, but I didn't have a way, so we went for a walk and made cocoa.

June 11th, 1952 - Dear Diary, I sure wished you had more room to write in. I finally got home after a bit of trouble and started washing.

June 12th, 1952 - Dear Diary, everybody is excited over fishing season. All the little boys are counting the days.

June 13th, 1952 - Dear Diary, I was asked to sing in church for a 4-H meeting. It's my big chance, but I don't know if I dare.

June 14th, 1952 - Dear Diary, we all went fishing today, and Daddy, Lincoln, Ikie, and Sam caught their limit. Roger was thrilled over his big one, but I just couldn't hook one.

June 15th, 1952 - Dear Diary, Jay and Mr. Christensen spoke today in meeting. It was very good, then I practiced my song and had a good visit with the folks.

June 16th, 1952 - Dear Diary, I went fishing again, and Karen and I caught a really big poling snag (what luck). I went down to practice and M.I.A.

Dear Diary, I guess I can't sing as good as I thought (which was a little). I was asked to sing "A Place in the Sun" for 4-H, and how on earth am I to learn it in a week with little or no way to practice the darn thing? I guess I shouldn't talk like this, but I just feel that way. How can I help but fail?

Allison has sweetly consented to help me if she can get a chance, and that means if Roy doesn't come down Tuesday, I just can't do it. You see, it's for Sunday, and I just don't know it.

June 17th, 1952 - Dear Diary, we met Uncle Cram's new wife today. I still haven't caught any fish, but I hope I can soon.

It might be o.k. I have been practicing, and maybe I can learn it.

June 18th, 1952 - I wish I could get into one of my good moods and want to write and really draw like I wanted to when I had a chance, but I wrote 2 poems.

Little Wanderer Rests

Trickle on little wandering stream.
Stop but one moment to catch the sun's beam.
Over all your rippling surface, let it spread its shining sheen
And hold in your depths its last golden gleam.

Trickle on little wandering stream.
Wind your way through departing days.
You have wandered late and long,
But your banks are still strong,
Nestled in their grassy green,
Fit enough for any queen.

Trickle on little wandering stream,
Down through the meadow flowered so gay
Where the little white lambs are at play.

Hurry on little wandering stream,
For the night is coming on.
But where little wanderer do you rest until dawn?

Like the baby lambs in the sweet green clover?
Or in a big red kennel like old Rover?

Or, little wandering stream, do you
Sleep in your meadow nook
By big Mama brook?
No, at the coming of dawn,
Like the little white lambs,
You join your mother stream
And go rushing on
To rest behind the big, big dams.

Our Longing

As we meet the trials and cares on this long journey,
There comes a weariness and longing for something we have not,
But all through the long day have sought.

Back to our childhood days we go, they so carefree and gay.
Then we could find a dear spot and dream there all day.

Then we could go from day to day
Without a fear or worry ever threatening our way.

It is those days we are longing for.
There was never a care our happiness to mar,
Or any uncertainly to leave its scar.

Along the rippling stream we linger where the grass is so green
And a tree points toward heaven its long green finger.
Here we could spend the day,
But our cares come calling us away.

Yes, we are longing for childhood days
To come back and replace these, our insecure grownup ways.

June 19th, 1952 - Dear Diary, I sure read a lot today. I found two good books with stories, so I really read. "Blue Melody" was the best.

June 20th, 1952 - Dear Diary, isn't a setting sun's last rays beautiful, especially up Liddy's Canyon? I went with them to milk.

June 21st, 1952 - Dear Diary, Clint Thompson and family came out today for a while. I saw "The Great Caruso," and I have never seen a better movie.

"The Great Couruso" was just wonderful, starring Maryo Lanza. It was about Caruso's life, most of it in grand opera, and can Maryo Lanza sing! All of that grand singing sure makes me certain I can't do anything, although I just dream of opera.

June 22nd, 1952 - Dear Diary, I guess it was o.k. I did sing it pretty good after all, although I could have done better.

June 23rd, 1952 - Dear Diary, I started cooking today and wrote letters and one was to a pen pal (2 years ago), Jo Ann Wright.

June 24th, 1952 - Dear Diary, we had 4-H here today, and I didn't get to M.I.A. I have been reading over some things I have written, talk about silliness!

June 25th, 1952 - Dear Diary, today Wendy and I tried making pedal pushers out of gunny sacks while Mama went to the ranch. It didn't work so well.

June 26th, 1952 - Dear Diary, I have decided to write to the Utah Farmers again and see if I can contribute a story. I need some money so I can try.

June 27th, 1952 - Dear Diary, I have begun to write "Song of Nature." I hope I can finish it for a book someday.

June 28th, 1952 - Dear Diary, how can a person write without paper? And, oh, I need a typewriter and lots of things. I would like to write so much.

June 29th, 1952 - Dear Diary, today Chick and Jean and the kids came to see us. Jean would like us to come and stay a while with her. Sammy and Lincoln are still to the ranch.

June 30th, 1952 - Dear Diary, I have been working outside today. It sure is better than cooking. I watered flowers and planted some too.

July 1st, 1952 - Dear Diary, I went to 4-H today and stayed to M.I.A. then Roy's and Allison's dance. It is sure different, Roy being married, but it is better for him.

July 2nd, 1952 - Dear Diary, today I worked, and am I tired! Tomorrow Clarissa, Pat, and family are coming for the 4th.

July 3rd, 1952 - Dear Diary, they didn't come today, and the kids aren't home yet, but they are going to get them for the 4th.

July 4th, 1952 - Dear Diary, our company finally came last night (awful late). Oh, but it has been a good day. Early this morning, we went to town to see the folks.

Then we went home for dinner. About 5:00, we went to the sports. We went home and got ready for a big picnic and roast that evening on our lawn with all of the folks.

Now let me tell you what was really fun. Lincoln and Wendy, Kenneth and me, and Jeremy and LeAnn all got ready for the dance at the open air dance. I wore my "dress" (the pink one), and Mama made me wear that corsage, but I didn't want to. We went in the Jeepster and what fun! We sang all the way down. When we got there, we danced and danced and had more fun. I hope Kenneth had as much fun as I did.

July 5th, 1952 - Dear Diary, I am so glad Aunt Clarissa and Uncle Pat and the kids could come down for a while, but they are leaving for Grand Canyon.

July 6th, 1952 - Dear Diary, today is the day we all go on the mountain. There was a little mix up, but I got there about 5:00.

July 7th, 1952 - Dear Diary, we have a nice camp by Wendy's, but we have no chaperone or teacher, so we do about what we want, and we have fun.

Well Dear Diary, guess who is here? Nathan, of all people to come on a 4-H trip. Why on earth did he have to come? Tonight I happened to see him at the skits, sitting over by Delbert, as happy as you please. I suddenly felt so dumb and mad too. I don't know why, but why did he have a right to come here?

July 8th, 1952 - Dear Diary, we had handy-craft today. I made a bracelet. We had M.I.A. too and a log sawing contest. Later we had skits.

Everybody got him to sign their paper on autographs, and Amy dared me to, so I decided to try it. He and Delbert were walking to handy-craft together, so I asked him and Delbert to sign it. Delbert did, and Nathan asked if he was to sign it too. I said go ahead, so he reluctantly signed it.

For something to say, I said, "You're taking 4-H this year?" That was a rather dumb thing to say.

"I wouldn't be up here if I wasn't," he barked as ornery as you please and acted as if he didn't know how to be sociable, to me that is. That put me in my place. I went over to handy-craft. Too bad he thinks I like him, so he has to show me he thinks I'm darn stupid, but I don't like him any more than he likes me, so there is no love lost. (He sure wrote his worst on my autograph).

July 9th, 1952 - Dear Diary, today we woke up to rain and more rain. We couldn't go on the nature hike, so we had our closing program and broke camp.

July 10th, 1952 - Dear Diary, today Uncle Pat and Kenneth and Jeremy left. Aunt Clarissa will leave on the 13th. Darn it! I wish they didn't have to leave.

July 11th, 1952 - Dear Diary, I helped decorate for the reception, and I am so happy because Aunt Lena and Curtis came and Aunt Lorraine and Jay.

July 12th, 1952 - Dear Diary, today we all got ready for Mary Alice's reception. My, but it was nice and so beautiful. Wendy was a bridesmaid, and I helped with the gifts.

July 13th, 1952 - Dear Diary, Lorraine and Jay and Clarissa and kids left today. Wendy went to Salt Lake. I am so glad she could go, but it will seem lonesome.

July 14th, 1952 - Dear Diary, Leana and Curtis stayed here for a while and then left this morning. It was so good to see them once again. I watered flowers.

July 15th, 1952 - Dear Diary, Mama and Daddy went to the St. George temple for the reunion. I tended the kids. Karen came up and helped.

July 16th, 1952 - Dear Diary, I am reading a very good book, "Q." I really like it. I weeded this evening and did some reading.

July 17th, 1952 - Dear Diary, really it seems like there isn't much I do anymore. I guess I am about to get lonesome. Lincoln and Sammy and Wendy and Johnny make a whole lot of difference, but I have been writing in my "novel." Ha! Ha!

July 19th, 1952 - Dear Diary, it makes you tired when you clean all of the house except two rooms, doesn't it? You see, Wendy isn't home yet.

July 20th, 1952 - Dear Diary, church was held in the evening tonight and Bro. Carol and one of the authorities from Kanab talked, and we were awarded certificates.

July 21st, 1952 - Dear Diary, I sent a poem and illustration into the Utah Farmer to see if I could win some money to pay for my permanent today.

July 22nd, 1952 - Dear Diary, I wanted to go to M.I.A. so much, but I didn't have a way down. You know Roy is married, and Daddy has to do the chores.

July 23rd, 1952 - Dear Diary, did I ever tell you about the art co.? They were going to send out their scout to look at my drawings. That would really be a chance for me wouldn't it? But Daddy wouldn't sign for it. He says they are just after my money, and we didn't have any! I would like to write my own "kid's stories" (stories for children) and draw for it.

July 25th, 1952 - Dear Diary, on the 24th we went to the ranch to see Lincoln and Sammy and have our lunch. It sure was a good time. Then we came home by Charles' way.

July 26th, 1952 - Dear Diary, way late, when we were all to bed, Wendy came in. She came on the bus, and it stopped right out front of our house.

July 27th, 1952 - Dear Diary, it is good to have her back. We went to Sunday school, and I was supposed to give a talk in meeting. I got there just in time.

Darn it, I still wish you had more room. Why don't you grow?

July 28th, 1952 - Dear Diary, it will be school pretty soon, and I am not ready for winter again. I am just scared to have school start again. I mean just (sort of) for a number of darn reasons.

July 29th, 1952 - Dear Diary, creeps! I asked Rita to come up today, and as luck would have it, I couldn't get down. Oh this business of transportation.

July 30th, 1952 - Dear Diary, I wrote "Canyon Music" from "Song of Nature" today, and we went to Dry Wash to shook grain. I tended Mary Ann.

Do you think I might have a chance? I sent "Our Longing" and "Canyon Music" to a book.

July 31st, 1952 - Dear Diary, I having read "Q," read "Riders Across the Border," then "Stone Desert." They weren't too good, but I got lonesome to read a book.

August 1st, 1952 - Dear Diary, well today is the first. I sure would like to go to Cedar, but I might not get to, it is so late.

August 2nd, 1952 - Dear Diary, all day long, in fact ever since I knew there was such a show as "Show Boat," I wanted to see it. It was excellent.

August 3rd, 1952 - Dear Diary, today Grandmother came to stay with us for a while. I got a letter from the "Utah Farmer," but no money.

August 4th, 1952 - Dear Diary, I guess I'm never going to earn money from writing, but I sure need some. But I hope to get a letter from the "17!" They will tell me how I rate anyway. I hope!

August 5th, 1952 - Dear Diary, we will probably have to forget about M.I.A. I guess. Transportation again.

August 6th, 1952 - Dear Diary, Wendy and I have been sleeping on the lawn, and Uncle Heber came, so Patricia will sleep with us. It was good to see them.

August 7th, 1952 - Dear Diary, Grandma left, and so did Uncle Heber, so our company is gone. Grandma wants us to come down.

August 8th, 1952 - Dear Diary, Mama and Daddy went to the ranch with Neldon and Eva, so I tended the kids. We went all over the hill.

August 9th, 1952 - Dear Diary, as usual, I cleaned house today. I want to go to Cedar, and Jean has invited me.

August 10th, 1952 - Dear Diary, I went to Sunday school today, but not to meeting. I read some good articles in the Relief Society magazine.

August 11th, 1952 - Dear Diary, I am getting ready to go to Cedar, if Daddy will let me go tomorrow with Aunt Eva.

August 24th, 1952 - My Dearest Diary, it is now the 24th. I have been gone for some time. I enjoyed my stay and learned to appreciate what I have. I may not have a beautiful rich home. A home that furnishes hard work and love, with companionship, is far better to me. I met people and saw things that might be called workable. They just made me love my people and my world. How I love the country.

I understand how so many can go astray, out where there are temptations and evils. It made me even feel different. It seemed good to get home again. I did go to a very good conference one Sunday, but also I went to some shows (later on in the week) that were not so good for me, that were rough ones with drinking. I may have gotten a bit home sick, but my it seemed good to be back home and go to conference.

August 21th, 1952 - Dear Diary, I remember we had a party (the Bullocks) the 21st. Jean wanted me to sing, so I did. Everyone made over my singing and said I was very good. I should not think so much of flattery, I guess, but I had wished they thought I was that good over here.

I wonder what this new school year will have for me.

August 24th, 1952 - Dear Diary, what a beautiful Sunday. I love a conference or good meeting more than most anything.

August 25th, 1952 - Dear Diary, Mama and I went to Springdale today to get peaches. I was very hot. Then Wendy went to Cedar.

August 26th, 1952 - Dear Diary, peaches, peaches. We have really worked them. I went to M.I.A. and really enjoyed it. It was "Treasures of Truth" night.

August 27th, 1952 - Dear Diary, school will soon be here again (oh dear), but we have a new music teacher and principal (oh goody).

August 28th, 1952 - Dear Diary, I have been trying to get ready for the fair. I have been sewing my 4-H things to enter them.

August 29th, 1952 - Dear Diary, I entered my things today. I am really discouraged about 4-H. I don't know what to do about it all.

August 30th, 1952 - Dear Diary, it was a nice fair, I guess, but I surely feel blue. My things didn't rate, and I'm worried about school.

August 31st, 1952 - Dear Diary, I am very glad we all have a Sunday and a chance to make it just what you need.

September 1st, 1952 - Dear Diary, gosh, summer is about gone, and I haven't done half of what I wanted to do.

September 2nd, 1952 - Dear Diary, today was Mama's birthday. Guess where we went? To the ranch, and I am sunburned.

It was so nice out there. I rode Doll and then rode her some more. Most of the leaves are changing.

September 4th, 1952 - Dear Diary, I am staying down at Croft's home to help out for a while. Hope I earn some money.

September 5th, 1952 - Dear Diary, I stayed with them today, and I will tomorrow too, and maybe after that.

September 6th, 1952 - Dear Diary, just think, school starts the 8th. I don't know if I want it to or not.

September 7th, 1952 - Dear Diary, I went to Sunday school today. Karen and Ora May are staying for a while. Aunt Eva is in Cedar.

September 8th, 1952 - Dear Diary, well school's here and the end of free sunny days, but let's make the best of it. I am staying down at Croft's until tomorrow (both Mon. and Tue.) nights. It is quite a good job, and I enjoy it.

September 10th, 1952 - Well Dear Diary, tonight is the first night I rode home on the bus, and it seems like we haven't had a break in school at all.

Ya know, I had the hardest time figuring out if I should take Algebra (a required subject) or if I should take Chorus (I'll tell you some more about it). Aunt Eva has had her baby, and it is a boy (goody).

Dear Diary, Ha! Here goes again. I guess it has been some time since I wrote you a note, but then school makes the difference. But don't get me wrong, I am in hopes I have one ounce of sense this year, but you can't ever tell about me, can you?

Maybe school won't be so bad.

Did I tell you of our new teachers, Mr. Hanson, the new principal, and Mr. Stocking? Guess what! The new music teacher. Oh, am I glad. Just think what that can mean to me, if I can sing? If I can prove it? If he thinks it? Mama said I am to take Vocal (gosh!),

My Dearest Diary

and Mr. Stocking says I can start Wednesday at 5:30. See, school might be good, and besides Mr. Stocking (I sure like him) says there is some kind of a music festival at Salt Lake (and a big chance). If I find out for sure, I will tell you all about it.

I take chorus (with about 43 others) under Mr. Stocking. He says we can have an opera, and he says we are very good. I hope we, and him too, won't be disappointed.

Could you be wondering how the case of (K.N.R.) or (S.N.N.) or just plain Nathan is coming along? Well first of all, I hope I am not so stupid. Things are about the same.

I believe you know what I said the day of the fair. Well, so long.

P.S. maybe I won't write all the particulars.

September 13th, 1952 - Dear Diary, I have been trying to make up for the Saturday I haven't been here. Boy! Am I tired tonight.

September 14th, 1952 - Dear Diary, what a fine Sunday I have had. I got to go to meeting (ward conference) and now Grandpa's.

September 15th, 1952 - Dear Diary, I am starting to realize school is starting. It seems all I can think of is singing or chorus and that application. But I feel blue tonight. I can't possibly be good enough to have a chance of winning (ha, ha).

I sat on the last seat in the bus. I was talking to Joy and the girls. Most of the seats were filled. Nathan (yes, that name again) found one by a girl, so he asked the girl just in front of me to trade him places (that was mean wasn't it?). Of course I talked all the harder and didn't notice him. He had to get in on the conversation, so he did. I set my sewing box and books on the seat.

Everybody talked some more, and soon the bus came to the first stop. My box toppled onto the floor and embroidery floss, cloth, and tape smattered all over. I hurried and picked them up. I noticed some cloth and embroidery floss was under Nathan's seat. I couldn't reach that far and pick it up. He started telling me about Alton's café and its wonders. I probably sounded as if I believed him. I don't know if I did or not. I saw my cloth and asked, "Will you pick that piece of cloth up for me?"

He colored a little, "If you'll say please."

"Please," I said. He picked up the cloth. I know he was the most embarrassed that time.

September 17th, 1952 - Dear Diary, guess what! I signed for the application and had my first lesson today. I hope I'm good enough!

Dear Diary, today I had my first lesson on Vocal. I will have it every Wednesday at 5:30, and I stayed at LeAnn's.

I can't help but worry about what Mr. Stocking thinks. It means so much to me, I mean the impression I make.

I will always want to remember today, my first lesson.

I was scared, and I really didn't do a lot, but I didn't have to sing or anything. It was on breathing.

September 18th, 1952 - Dear Diary, remember "Our Longing," a poem I wrote? Well, Mrs. Bauer wants me to get Mr. Stocking to help me with it.

September 19th, 1952 - Dear Diary, today I went to Kanab to watch the first football game. We were really beat, but anyway, we tried.

September 20th. 1952 - Dear Diary, I went to the dance tonight. There wasn't many there, but it was pretty good.

Wendy is to Logan on an F.H.A. trip.

September 21st. 1952 - Oh! Dear Diary, it was the best meeting today. Mr. Christensen and Mr. Stocking talked.

September 22nd, 1952 - Dear Diary, about all I can think about and worry about right now is singing. I mean almost.

September 23rd, 1952 - Dear Diary, I get to go to Salt Lake and sing in the tabernacle. Just imagine!!

Dear Diary, guess what?? Things are really happening. I get to go to the all-state chorus (aren't you glad for me?). If I can only learn the music in 2 weeks (I believe I will go, that is). Tomorrow I have to sing in my lesson. Gosh, a lot depends on that (wish me luck).

Well I was scared, of course. I tried "Anne Laurey," and he said I had good tones.

September 24th, 1952 - Dear Diary, I stayed down at Rita's so I could take my lesson and other things. I have been asked to sing on Friday.

September 25th, 1952 - Dear Diary, we had a Seminary party today. I really had fun. We had a melon bust and games.

September 26th, 1952 - Dear Diary, I sang "Half as Much" today in the opening assembly. I did last year too.

Did I tell you about Friday? I still don't know if he likes me or not, he was very attentive until I stood up to sing. All at once he had to fight with Gerald or do something. Criminy!! And Steven put his hands to his ears.

I got off pitch or something and didn't get going until the song was half over.

September 27th, 1952 - Dear Diary, I have been cleaning house today. Monday I have to start on "Freshie week."

September 28th, 1952 - Dear Diary, I went to Sunday school, but I had to tend the kids during meeting, so I missed it.

September 29th, 1952 - Dear Diary, I had to wear a beanie (a hat) today. I don't especially like it.

September 30th, 1952 - Dear Diary, I wore missed matched stockings and a beanie today. I stayed to teach the Relief Society kids.

I went to an assembly.

September 31st, 1952 - Guess what? Nathan thinks Deanna is tops, (she is the most popular girl in school). She is a cheerleader and today was put up for F.F.A. queen. Well, let him think it. See who cares. Tomorrow, we have to wear our boyfriend's name around our neck. Everybody thinks I'm putting (Nathan). Well, they'll find out different!! Don't you think I have a little pride?

October 1st, 1952 - Dear Diary, I wore one earring, a beanie, and missed matched socks today.

I put Steven's name and am I glad. Nathan acted kind of surprised. "Well, my dear boy, did you think I was head over heels for you?" You better learn different, Mr. Roberts. Yah know, I like Steven. He's a pretty good guy.

October 2nd, 1952 - Dear Diary, I wore all of the things I did yesterday and Steven's name on a card around my neck – it was commanded.

October 3rd, 1952 - Dear Diary, what a day (Freshie Day) and our dance, "What a Night" our theme was.

Dear Diary, I am for sure going up to Salt Lake. I have my music and will go up next Wednesday. I am so glad. I am taking lessons and trying to learn how to sing.

Subject changed.

My Dear Diary, Nathan goes around and acts like he was everything and shows off (oh, he's ornery).

Tonight we were all ready for the bus for our dance (Freshie Frolic). The moon was big and full, so we were dancing around on the lawn, when down the road came a pickup, and as it passed us the dear driver honked to let us know he was off for his queen – Criminy! When we were at the dance, and I was about to go in with Lincoln, Steven asked where my date was. I pointed to Lincoln. Maybe he wanted me to go with him because he danced with me three times and sat by me going home. I danced with Lincoln and had a good time.

I'm glad Nathan was too busy with his popular Deanna to dance with me. I would have been tempted to turn him down. I wish I didn't like his looks and voice so well, but I'll get over it if he keeps acting like he does.

October 4th, 1952 - Dear Diary, today was Lincoln's 17th birthday. My big brother is really growing up.

October 7th, 1952 - Dear Diary, I am busy getting ready to go to Salt Lake. I'm sure excited. See you when I get back.

October 8th, 1952 - Dear Diary, we went to Salt Lake City and registered at West High School and had our first practice.

Dear Diary, we left at about 11:30 to go to Salt Lake. There was my cousin, Yvonne Cornellia, and Dale Heaton and all of the Stocking family. We had a wonderful trip. We stopped at the Big Rock Mountain and didn't get to Aunt Clarissa's until about 10:35. Yvonne and I stayed there. I saw a so-called T.V. for the first time. It was sure interesting, but maybe not all too good for me. As soon as we got there, we went to the West High School to get registered and have our first practice.

Mr. Newell B. White was our director and, my, he is good. Why, he was just perfect. He really knew what he was doing, and he was so humorous we couldn't help but like him. He could get and keep our attention and have us do just what he wanted us to do (he was very nice looking too). He teaches at the B.Y.U. I would sure like to take music under him.

There were 350 in the chorus. Oh, but it was just grand!! Thursday we practiced twice for about two hours at a time, and I enjoyed every minute of it, especially on "Good News" and "Comin' Through the Rye." Yvonne and I walked all over and spent most of the day in the city, then Mr. Stocking would take us home.

October 9th, 1952 - Dear Diary, we practiced today and walked, it seemed like, all over Salt Lake.

October 10th, 1952 - Dear Diary, today I must remember as one of the best in my whole life (All State Chorus).

Dear Diary, Friday (the big day) finally came. We went to town and had two more practices before 5:00, then we began our concert. 1. "Praise We Sing to Thee" 2. "Sweet and Low" 3. "Good News" 4. "Lord, to Thee Our Hearts Are Raised" 5. "Comin' through the Rye" 6. "Fierce was the Wild Billow." The all state orchestra played: 7. "A Mighty Fortress is our God."

My, but it gave me a thrill. It was the most wonderful thing that has ever happened to me.

Right after our program, we saw and heard Ike talk. We couldn't get back into the tabernacle, so we watched it over T.V. in the assembly hall.

And I will always remember too how we rushed to the tabernacle and saw the one who was the most important to us, President David O. McKay. I have never seen such fine expressions. Everyone was trying to get his autograph, and he was in a hurry, so I just stood where I could have touched his shoulder and watched him. He is a very wonderful man. I'm glad I got to see him. Outside we met Mr. White and got his autograph.

That was a wonderful day and night for me (the most wonderful). Temple square was lit up so beautifully, and it seemed so like a quiet garden spot guarded from a noisy city.

October 11th, 1952 - Dear Diary, I went to the capital, the historical building, and tried to eat some Chinese food today.

Kenneth took us to the capital and around Salt Lake.

October 12th, 1952 - Dear Diary, today ended our trip with wonderful things to think of.

We came home. We saw the lovely Manti temple that night when it was all lit up, and when I got home at 11:30, I knew I had a lot of loveliness to remember.

October 13th, 1952 - Dear Diary, it seems like I haven't been to school for days and days, but it seems good.

October 15th, 1952 - Dear Diary, I had my music lesson today. It was on tone resonates (I better practice more).

October 16th, 1952 - Dear Diary, I hope now I can settle down and study. I don't think I have a chance in the opera.

October 17th, 1952 - Dear Diary, today was the F.F.A. assembly (guess who sang?). The Deer Hunter's Ball was tonight, but I didn't go.

October 18th, 1952 - Dear Diary, I did house work today.
Did I ever tell you about getting a letter from "17?" They encouraged me.

October 19th, 1952 - Dear Diary, church was good today. I went to Sunday school and meeting.

October 20th, 1952 - Dear Diary, we don't go to school today or tomorrow because school was let out for deer hunting.

October 21st, 1952 - Dear Diary, today we all sorted pants and worked around the house.

October 22nd, 1952 - Dear Diary, Mr. Stocking asked me to sing "Hill of Home." I'll try it, but it will be hard. I sure get discouraged sometimes about my vocal and realize I am dumber than I thought, that I wonder if it's worth it, but maybe someday I can learn how to be better.
Lincoln says I've got the looks enough to be one of the most popular girls in the school, but I haven't the intelligence. Well, I know how to act, but I just can't do it.

October 28th, 1952 - Dear Diary, today is Michael's birthday.

October 29th, 1952 - Dear Diary, tonight I stayed down to Rita's. Saturday I am going to sing "Hills of Home," so I practiced.

October 30th, 1952 - Dear Diary, I got a dollar from "The Utah Farmer" on a drawing of a dog house. It was kind of funny.

October 31st, 1952 - Dear Diary, I will have to tell you about the opera. I am quite sure I will be in it.

November 1st, 1952 - Dear Diary, I'm Natalie (yahoo!). Goody, goody! We practice every day (just the seven of us). It's sure fun, but darn it! I can't give of myself like I should. I'm too self-conscious and nervous and dumb. Maybe someday it will be different. Why is it I can't be more friendly and more popular? I guess I better try, try, and try again. Sometimes I am all right, then I lock up in myself and just ruin it. Sometimes I remind myself of Melissa, a character in a book called "Melissa," only I hope I'm not like Melissa was. It was kind of funny the other day. I laughed right out loud as Jim (Richard) turned and stared at me, then Mr. Stocking was saying how I should get expression in my song, then people will say, "Well, she isn't dead after all."

Dear Diary, we are putting on an operetta. The main parts are: Natalie, Richard, and Colonel. Yvonne was to be Natalie, but she is sick. Elaine didn't think she could do it, so I get to be Natalie if she doesn't get better. But I do hope she gets better. Jim is Richard. Lincoln is Colonel. Nathan is Franklyn, and I was to be Marbell (opposite Nathan – poor Nathan).

There is to be an F.H.A. Girls' Date Dance next Friday. Guess who I would like to take? Bob, but it is probably impossible.

November 8th, 1952 - Dear Diary, believe it or not, I went to the dance, but I suffered from it. I caught an awful cold.

Dear Diary, it's Friday today and what a mix up! Rita and I were going to get a date with the boys from Orderville, and I would stay down. But Johnny turned down Rita, and Lavoy wouldn't say anything but, "I don't like to go to dances." And when Rita asked Duane to go, he wouldn't give his answer. I waited for Duane to consent before I asked Lavoy again or possibly Bob.

November 9th, 1952 - Dear Diary, I had to stay home all day today because of this darn cold, and I had to miss singing in conference.

November 10th, 1952 - Dear Diary, it seems like I haven't been to school for a week, but I enjoy reading "Ben Hur." It's awful good.

November 11th, 1952 - Dear Diary, it really is fun putting on that opera! I just hope I can make a success of it. "Oh, boy!"

November 12th, 1952 - Dear Diary, I sure can get down-hearted sometimes. One day I'm ok, and the next day I lose out again, but wish me luck for tomorrow.

November 13th, 1952 - Dear Diary, the opera went off fine, and I think we all enjoyed it. I'm sure enthused about studying now.

My, Dear Diary, we had the opera today! I could have sung "Just a Song at Twilight" better, and when I sat down (like he was supposed to do) Jim took my hand. I didn't think he would, and I blushed. Then he said, "You're not afraid of me are you?" And criminy, I blushed! But other than that (I guess that was alright anyway), I did alright until I left out one speech, but it wasn't very important.

I was really complimented, and it's been a wonderful day! I'm looking forward to putting it on in costume and on stage at Alton. It really is only about 20 minutes long and not much of a story, but it is an opera and a start for me (I hope).

Remember, Dear Diary, last year how I wanted to be in an opera? Well I got my wish, but maybe not at the right time. I sang a solo and sang with Jim "In the Glooming." You know Jim, the most popular and well-liked by all the girls. He's a Junior. But now it's too late for me to do anything, and now tonight is the dance, and I have to stay home and tend Mary Ann. I can't ask Bob at the last minute anyway, so I guess I stay home. Remember last girls' day dance? By the way Nathan is going with Carol Jean. (This isn't the real girls' day dance, it's the Sadie Hawkins Day dance, without costume).

Well I did go to the dance, but I didn't ask Nathan to dance. Should I have? Don't tell anybody, but I just can't help liking him, darn it! And I am mean for thinking this, but I am glad I'm opposite Jim, and LeAnn still likes him. She came to me and praised me. What I'm really thrilled about is getting a main part in a "wonderful" opera. Did I tell you we may put it on in costume on stage in Alton? The 13th we put it on at the school. I just hope I can act well enough.

November 14th, 1952 - Dear Diary, we did not go to school today, it was parents' day. I read in "The Light Heart," and I had better settle down and study more in school. I believe I got just one A this term. The others were B's.

November 16th, 1952 - Dear Diary, I would sure like to get A's again. Don't mean to brag, but I used to get better grades.

November 17th, 1952 - Dear Diary, guess what? I was called out of the audience to sing "Irish eyes are Smiling." "The Chimers" presented a show for us, and I was asked to sing to their accompaniment!

November 18th, 1952 - Dear Diary, what if I got a chance to take piano lessons? Maybe I have, with Mrs. Lafever.

November 26th, 1952 - Dear Diary, sometimes I get so discouraged. Tomorrow is Thanksgiving, so today we celebrated. We had a school dance. It started off being fun. I luckily got out on the dance floor, and I danced with Lincoln. I really like to dance with him, and I usually can, pretty good. Then I got in a circle dance, but somehow ended up with Nathan. The music stopped when he was my partner. He had really been dancing (it was hot), and I have never seen anybody sweat like he did, and he looked down at the floor and acted like he was going to faint (and not because he ended out with me either, I hope). He didn't act as if I was anybody or anything. I wonder if you know what I mean.

I said something, but I can't remember what it was. "Do we dance?" is what he said (unconcerned you know) – and I said, "I guess." Well, we started to dance. I did my best to follow him. I hadn't danced with him for so long, and I'm such a _____ of a dancer (darn it). I resolve to learn to dance, before I ever try it again and make a fool of myself. So you can't (or can you?) blame him when after only ½ of a minute, he said "Let's catch up with Ted." I didn't know what for, and he said to Ted, "I'll trade you." What more could Ted do but accept the struggle. Then he said, "Let's change."

Woe is me! Didn't I feel nice. But before we could, somebody clapped for Ted. That was a little bit of an embarrassment. I felt horrible and went in the dressing room (of all people). I didn't even want any candy they had at the last of the dance. I just wanted to come home and make up my mind to learn how to dance. And by darn, I've got to if I'm ever to be anybody. Why is it that most people can fit in with the music and dance with anybody and others just positively can't? It doesn't seem fair. And you just have to be able to dance.

November 30th, 1952 - Happy Thanksgiving!

December 26th, 1952 - Dear Diary, I should be ashamed of myself. I haven't written for 27 days, but it seems as if I just couldn't get around to it. Let's see, where should I start? Where I left off? Well, we had a good Thanksgiving, and we do have a lot to be thankful for. I hope we can pay Dola part of what she demands. And guess what? Somebody likes Janet really well and courts her in style, but I shouldn't feel bad! Didn't I decide I didn't like him? You know, he's about to be like Jim, in more ways than one, and so he is so far above me. He thinks (I guess).

I had the three day measles or something for a while. Then I was asked to sing "O Little Town of Bethlehem" in church. I could have done better, I know, but I was complimented by quite a few people, and it was the people who counted, by the bishop, his councilors, and the townspeople. Christmas is always a worry, but I managed to get a few things, and afterward we had an assembly (I sang "Silver Bells). Tuesday, we were let out of school.

Yesterday was a fine Christmas for all of us. I feel so lucky to have so many brothers and sisters, even if they wake me up at 12:00 and yell, "Is it morning?" At 5:00, we were woken again, and once we got up (Me and Wendy) we just couldn't go back to bed again. It seemed like I just don't have any clothes, so I was glad to get a sweater and other clothes, and I got two jars of shampoo (you see Daddy doesn't like it, so we have a hard time getting it). You can see I was glad to get some for a gift. I went to the show "Westward the Women" last night. It wasn't too good. But I was curious to see it because some local people were in it, and it was filmed around in our Kane County.

I went to the last of the Christmas dance. I was so tired, I sighed with relief when it was over. It's funny, but I don't seem to hate sitting on the bench so much as I use to, and I don't let things bother me so much. I guess it's because I don't have a case on anybody (I mean have a boyfriend). So many of the girls do. Sometimes I think, well I shouldn't feel bad because I'm not so called popular. I'm well-liked by most everybody. And maybe it wouldn't be so good for me to have boyfriends and all of that. Don't they usually cause too many worries? And I have decided dancing is not all there is and that is not my talent. It would be nice to know how, and maybe I will really learn how to someday.

But in the meantime, I will try to be kind and friendly to everyone and learn more about singing, writing, and drawing so someday I will be recognized and loved. I want so much to learn and to do things. I think I live in the future too much, Dear Diary, and I hope you will remind me to keep studying now and being friends today and maybe tomorrow I will be the woman I want to be. I guess I had better stop writing and go to bed before I use all of the space and time.

December 30th, 1952 - Dear Diary, today it was like spring, and I climbed the hill and gathered gum. Yesterday was Wendy's birthday (16th).

December 31st, 1952 - It snowed last night. Tonight we had an M.I.A. New Year party. It was really fun. Well, Happy New Year!

Memorandum

Dear Diary, I hope I am learning more this year. I realize already how silly I must have sounded when I first started writing. I hope I am improving. I will soon be 15.

CATHY CORNELLIA

1953

January 1st, 1953 - Today we have really celebrated, Dear Diary. We made ice cream, cookies, and cooked chicken and had a big family dinner.

January 2nd, 1953 - Dear Diary, tonight was the Seniors' dance. Don't tell anybody, but I only danced with Lincoln. I wonder if I'll ever dance more.

January 3rd, 1953 - Dear Diary, today I cleaned house and mopped floors. I'm rather tired.

January 4rd, 1953 - Dear Diary, today was a very good Sunday. Meeting was wonderful. We had a party at Uncle Logan's tonight.

January 5th, 1953 - Dear Diary, we had to go back to school again (darn it). I am reading a book Veronica gave me, "The Master's Violin."

January 6th, 1953 - Dear Diary, I should worry more about my music, or that is remember to practice and improve it. I sure hate to start school again because it's such nice weather, and I get spring fever and want to climb the hills. On Christmas, I was lonesome for the ranch. It really hasn't snowed like it did last year. We had a ballgame with Dixie tonight, and we beat them by 13 points. That's pretty good, don't you think?

January 10th, 1953 - Dear Diary, I cleaned house as usual today. Do you think I'm as silly as I was last year? I hope not.

January 11th, 1953 - Dear Diary, today is Sunday. We had a very good meeting. This afternoon, Grandpa and Becca came from Dixie to see us.

January 12th, 1953 - Dear Diary, school is pretty good, and I hope I'm learning more about English because if I ever write I will have to know it.

January 13th, 1953 - Dear Diary, tonight we had quite a time. Well you know the truck, no windshield wiper, no window in the right door, a wobbly rock with a lean to it, and tonight no battery or lights. Daddy wasn't anxious that we go to M.I.A. because it was raining quite hard. We would have to start on a hill and the street was running with water, but Wendy and I had parts on the M.I.A. program, and Daddy didn't say no!

After rolling the truck down the drive, we (Lincoln and Wendy) climbed in and started off. We could hardly see, the rain was pouring down, it was dark, the lights were dim, and we had no windshield wiper, but Lincoln did have a handkerchief. I felt scared and like we were going on some dangerous but exciting trip. Lincoln tried to shift gears and the truck groaned, but the shift acted as if it were stuck. I was holding Ikie and thought our legs were in the way but instead the breaks were on. Then the side lights flickered and went out. We drove on to the garage, and Lincoln pulled off the road. Finally, after flicking the lights for a few minutes, he convinced them to stay on, and we started out again. Slowly, we made our way through Glendale.

I don't know what the others were thinking, but I was imagining all sorts of things. We barely crept over the road, and as we crossed the bridge about ¾ miles out of Glendale, the lights grew dimmer. Around the corner came a car, and I knew Lincoln couldn't see much. Quickly, he tried to turn off the road, and the car whizzed by. We were left in utter darkness. The battery was dead. I wasn't surprised. I think we were all expecting it. Lincoln started for Glendale, and Wendy stood in the rain, flashing the flashlight to warn oncoming cars. Thank goodness for the flashlight. The truck was on about half of the road. Ikie was saying if a diesel came, we would be crushed and so would it.

Three cars stopped and asked if we needed help, and Wendy explained. The rain kept pattering on the road, and we waited. A big truck finally came, and Lincoln, Norman, and Vance jumped out with a chain. Soon, we were home, and the big diesel came roaring down the road (but darn it, we didn't make it to M.I.A. after all).

January 15th, 1953 - Dear Diary, I was supposed to take my lesson today, right after school, so I could go home on the bus. Mr. Stocking had me practice.

January 17th, 1953 - Dear Diary, today was not an ordinary Saturday. Guess what!?! We got a new car, a Chevrolet, although a 1940 make.

January 18th, 1953 - Dear Diary, I suppose you remember Nathan. He's rather ignorant. I decided I'd tell you, so you would know. It wasn't much, but it makes me think he is not quite as handsome as he thinks he is. He happened to sit in front of me. We had to pass a moving house and the bus would have to go around it. It sounds pretty dumb, but I just didn't think, and I said, "This makes me scared." He turned around and with that catty I-think-you're-dumb look on his face, he said, "Yah, I'll bet you're scared to death." When he made a bright remark, I wanted to tell him the same thing back, but I couldn't. But don't think I won't. I make some remark, so he has to smother it to make me feel like I'm a nobody and to show me he doesn't think I'm so hot! But Nathan just you wait!!

January 18th, 1953 - Dear Diary, I surely enjoy Sundays. Today I read in "The Pearl of Great Price." It is very interesting.

January 19th, 1953 - Dear Diary, we had a party for my birthday tonight in Home Evening. Daddy told us stories and experiences, and we all had a very good time to remember.

January 20th, 1953 - Dear Diary, I have had a very happy birthday. I received some gifts and saw a show in school.

January 21st, 1953 - Dear Diary, the flu is sure going around. It seems as if everyone is sick. It was so bad they almost let school out.

January 22nd, 1953 - Dear Diary, Wendy is staying at Orderville with Chad and LeAnn. I stayed home with the flu.

January 23rd, 1953 - Dear Diary, today I wrote some more on that novel I'm trying to write, but it seems as if I still don't do it correctly.

January 24th, 1953 - Dear Diary, I stayed at Lafever's and tended their boys while they went to the ballgame at Cedar. We were beat by 16 points.

January 25th, 1953 - Dear Diary, I went to church today. I surely am getting tired of school. I don't know why, but I've lost all of my ambition. Maybe it was the flu.

January 26th, 1953 - Dear Diary, back to school again. There is a new student teacher teaching Ag. for a term. He is very young. His name is Ains.

January 27th, 1953 - Dear Diary, tonight is M.I.A. We danced. It was a lot of fun. Guess who was to M.I.A.?

January 28th, 1953 - Dear Diary, today we had a first practice on the play we plan to present for our assembly. I didn't take my music lesson.

January 29th, 1953 - Dear Diary, I went to Kanab today to see the doctor about fixing my glasses. I only missed a half a day's school.

January 30th, 1953 - Dear Diary, we beat Kanab in basketball tonight. I believe it was the best game I have been to.

January 31st, 1953 - Dear Diary, I cleaned house today, as usual.

February 1st, 1953 - Dear Diary, I went to Sunday school, and this evening I went to Lydie's canyon and finished "The Pearl of Great Price." It was very good.

February 2nd, 1953 - Dear Diary, we sure haven't had much snow this winter, and now it seems like spring.

February 3rd, 1953 - Dear Diary, I went to the Speech Festival that we had in place of M.I.A. in the church house. My, it was good.

February 4th, 1953 - Dear Diary, there is not much that happens in school anymore. I just study hard (sometimes).

February 6th, 1953 - Dear Diary, most everyone went to the Hurricane game down there, but I didn't. We were beaten. Tomorrow will be conference at Kanab, and we will sing in one meeting.

February 8th, 1953 - Dear Diary, the meetings were very good, and I guess the songs went over o.k., but we were about left over there.

February 9th, 1953 - Dear Diary, this is going to be a busy week. We are having our 9th assembly, and Saturday is the Gold and Green Ball.

February 10th, 1953 - Dear Diary, we have partly postponed our assembly until next Friday. Thank goodness.

February 11th, 1953 - Dear Diary, I have just got to learn to sing (like I mean it) with more expression. I can feel it, but sometimes I'm just too self-conscious. Mr. Stocking says to "enjoy myself more," and that is what Mama says too.

February 13th, 1953 - Dear Diary, I am in the floor show tomorrow night for the dance, and Mama is making me a pink formal.

February 14th, 1953 - Dear Diary, it was a good dance. There was a good crowd, and our dance turned out ok (but of course I didn't dance much, as usual).

February 15th, 1953 - Dear Diary, I just love Sundays. I won't know what we would do without them. I went to church and prayed in Sunday School.

February 16th, 1953 - Dear Diary, tomorrow we will go to a meeting given on "fabrics." It seems nobody likes the teachers anymore, and I wonder if the school isn't a little bit too disrespectful.

February 18th, 1953 - Dear Diary, in P.E. class we had a big fight. Some kids are certainly ignorant, disrespectful, and ornery.

February 19th, 1953 - Dear Diary, I had sort of a fight with Eva and Betty, but you would too.

My Dearest Diary

February 20th, 1953 - Dear Diary, I sang "Lady of Spain" in our assembly. Tonight I tended kids. It surely has been a day!

February 21st, 1953 - Dear Diary, I sang (in between acts) tonight in a play from Kanab. I sang "Lady of Spain." It seems that's all I do sing.

February 22nd, 1953 - Dear Diary, meeting was surely good. Virgil is back from his mission and he gave a talk in meeting and at a fireside at Jeremy's.

February 23rd, 1953 - Dear Diary, the wind has blown all day, and it is getting cold again. We may have more winter. Tonight we practiced for M.I.A.

February 24th, 1953 - Dear Diary, I am so thankful for our family. We all went to M.I.A. tonight. It was really quite an experience. We presented the program.

February 25th, 1953 - Dear Diary, I still must practice more and work harder in my music. I do not sing distinctly enough and with enough force.

February 26th, 1953 - Dear Diary, a cold caught me again, and I stayed home from school. "The Silver Chalice" is a very good book to read.

March 1st, 1953 - Dear Diary, today was a good Sunday.

March 2nd, 1953 - Dear Diary, I did not go to school today. I have a cold, and I am sick. I believe I am missing more school this year.

March 3rd, 1953 - Dear Diary, tomorrow is the Ward Reunion. It should be a big day. Everyone who has ever lived in Orderville is invited.

March 4th, 1953 - Dear Diary, it was an eventful day! I met lots of folks and enjoyed programs, dancing, and a banquet.

March 5th, 1953 - Dear Diary, tomorrow is Mary Ann's 2nd birthday.

March 6th, 1953 - Dear Diary, I went to the game at Kanab. It was very exciting. We won twice, about 23 to 44 and 15 to 25.

March 7th, 1953 - Dear Diary, I'm sure tired today. Wendy went to an F.H.A. meeting, and I did more work.

March 8th, 1953 - Dear Diary, I went to Sunday school (we all did). Mary Ann had a very good birthday. She and Mama went to Cedar.

March 9th, 1953 - Dear Diary, it seems different now that Mama is not home.

March 10th, 1953 - Dear Diary, Mama came back today.

March 11th, 1953 - Dear Diary, today was the Solos and Ensembles (I guess I didn't make the grade again).

March 12th, 1953 - Dear Diary, today I gave Rita a birthday present, a homemade handkerchief.

March 13th, 1953 - Dear Diary, Sammy came down with the Chicken Pox. There was a game with Kanab (they won).

March 14th, 1953 - Dear Diary, I am reading the "Mysterious Rider." I don't know if it is good or not.

March 15th, 1953 - Dear Diary, oh, we had a good meeting tonight. Howard reported from his mission.

March 16th, 1953 - Dear Diary, we are trying to learn a new dance, and boy if it isn't hard. It is fast and with ballet steps.

March 17th, 1953 - Dear Diary, in M.I.A. tonight we had a very good program, and in class we opened the question box.

March 18th, 1953 - Dear Diary, I am not doing enough in music. It seems I am not progressing enough. I did not have my lesson again.

March 19th, 1953 - Dear Diary, Friday we had a very good assembly. It was on family problems, prejudices, and friendliness.

March 21th, 1953 - Dear Diary, I had to stay home again. The folks went to a F.F.A. banquet. I finished my story "Great Ships" tonight.

March 22nd, 1953 - Dear Diary, I believe we had a better meeting tonight than ever before. The bishopric was reorganized.

March 23rd, 1953 - Dear Diary, I read my story today. Mr. Bauer thought it was very good. He really complimented me.

March 24th, 1953 - Dear Diary, I read my story to the Juniors (Mr. Bauer's orders). Guess what? He marked it A+. Oh goody. It took some work, but it was worth it. I read it to the 8th grade too. Gwenda and Rita read theirs too.

March 26th, 1953 - Dear Diary, I guess I don't get to dance in Fredonia after all. I am to be in another square.

March 27th, 1953 - Dear Diary, in school today the 8th grade had their assembly, and we had a matinee dance (unlucky). Well, I didn't even get to go to the Gold and Green ball at Fredonia. Wendy and Lincoln didn't get back from the Speech Festival.

March 29th, 1953 - Dear Diary, I went to Sunday school but had to tend the kids for meeting. They really have chicken pox.

March 30th, 1953 - Dear Diary, it snowed this morning, but when I came home from school, it was as green and fresh as ever.

April 1st, 1953 - Dear Diary, today is April Fool's Day, and I and Arleen sang "If I Were the Only Girl in the World" in the F.H.A. play.

April 2nd, 1953 - We also sang it on Thursday (today April 2nd). It was quite fun
   Dear Diary, some people from U.S.A.C. gave a musical assembly. It was just wonderful. Beth really sings.

April 3rd, 1953 - We surely had a good assembly today – but let me tell you about the Sophomores' (Wendy's) dance. Of course we are low on money, but we thought we could go, and I wanted to awfully bad (imagine!). Well I hadn't been to a dance for a long time, and I had a new skirt. Daddy didn't have any money, and we could only find 26 cents. We thought Daddy might get some from town, but he didn't. To add to our troubles, the water wouldn't run because the tank was not filled. We really felt the blues.
   Finally, Wendy and I washed, and she planned to see if she couldn't get into her own dance free and gave me the 25 cents. We hurried and ran out to wait for the bus. Well, we waited for a half hour or more and still no bus. A car drove up and asked if we wanted to go to the dance with them. They were Arlene's folks. We piled in, and that made 12 people in one car. Ten kids came from Alton. A tight squeeze? Ha, ha. We found out the bus driver had forgotten about the dance – and there were some mad Sophomores that night. Well, the dance was the same for me, only Lincoln wasn't there so -----.

I sat back and watched a Junior dance close to all of the girls. (for disgusting). He was what you might call a "flirt." Beginning to grow up makes a difference (I guess).

April 4th, 1953 - Dear Diary, today is Roger's birthday so we had a big dinner and party for Easter too! Eva and Neldon came up, and we had a good time. Sunday was a fine Easter too. We went to church.

April 6th, 1953 - Dear Diary, it is just another Monday. Time to worry about the lack of money.

April 7th, 1953 - Dear Diary. I went to M.I.A. We will soon have a "Rose Prom."

April 8th, 1953 - Dear Diary, I sure feel blue. It is all over this business of cash (the lack of it I mean).

I'm broke. I mean we're broke.

How can a person wash her hair in soot? In the spring, with all of its activities and going-ons, I feel I just have to have something. I charge for what I feel I just have to have, but where is the marker? Yesterday I was asked to sing a song in a meeting for tomorrow. I just ticked material for the clothes I was required to make in school, and I have to have a dress for an all girls dance. We are trying to sell candy for that. Today I was supposed to buy (after school) more sugar for more candy, but I had to take a lesson so the money was left in the locker.

Wendy stayed for primary. I came home and started on the dress I hoped to have for tomorrow night. She was mad about the money and told me I had the dress sewed wrong. I hoped to have things ready for tomorrow, and I planned to wash my head and polish my shoes. I almost sweared when I found there was no (Tide) soap, let alone shampoo, in the house and still no shoe polish. Lincoln was going downtown to get Wendy and try to get the money from the locker, so I wrote a note (soap, vinegar, sugar, shoe polish).

They had a fit. We couldn't possibly get them. I had been polishing my shoes with soot, and Mama said it would have to do. Daddy was not in the house, but still I couldn't resist asking for shampoo. "I was going to sing." They said we could not have any. Maybe they wouldn't let us charge Tide. Then I pleaded (and believe me, I pleaded) for some vinegar, but no, we could not afford any. "Well," I said, "do I have to wash my hair in soot too?" It just doesn't seem fair. No shoe polish, no shampoo, just no nothing.

I've been bawling for an hour. I haven't bawled for a long, long time, and I daren't go downstairs.

April 9th, 1953 - Dear Diary, I really made a mess of that song. I feel terrible! I did not know it well enough.

Dear Diary, I was asked to sing a song for a program in Glendale. I tried to sing "The Dickey Bird Song," and I didn't know it, so I made an awful mess.

April 10th, 1953 - Dear Diary, today was V day and the time to clean up the school, then tonight was a V dance.

Today was V day. I helped clean the Seminary building. It was a lot of fun. In the afternoon was a track meet. Lincoln won the one mile race and throwing the javelin.

April 11th, 1953 - Dear Diary, we 9th graders went to the temple today and were baptized ten times for the dead.

Dear Diary, last night I stayed at Rita's for the "Rose Prom." We got to sleep around 12:30 and left for St. George about 6:30 or so the next morning.

Does a sleeping party after a dance and the night before going to the temple sound familiar? We had a very nice time. I was baptized ten times. After lunch we went to the airport and Santa Clara, visited about all of the stores, and window shopped. On the way home, we walked through the tunnel, and in Springdale we saw the Arts and Crafts shop. It was a very interesting and exciting day, but not until we got home did we realize how tired we were.

April 12th, 1953 - Dear Diary, today I went to three meetings: Sunday school, testimony meeting, and an award meeting.

April 13th, 1953 - Dear Diary, it's back to school again, and I am still tired from Saturday. I planted some flowers today.

April 14th, 1953 - Dear Diary, I feel awful about that song, and I was asked to sing for the Girls' Day Assembly, so I decided I will try to sing it again and this time learn to sing it right. I'm getting tired of singing, and I don't practice like I should. I guess you wonder what I am going to do for the Girls' Day Dance. Well, so do I!

April 17th, 1953 - Dear Diary, it has been a big day. I guess my song went all right. I was really scared. And the dance? I didn't have half the anxiety I did last year. I didn't ask anybody, so I went with Lincoln. It was Wendy who had the worries. She asked Mark Pine. He consented, but there were the transportation troubles. There was a mix up, and it ended up with Lincoln and me in the front seat and Mark and Wendy in the back seat of our car at about 10:00, or an hour after the dance, but all ended well.

I danced every dance but two or three, and I could follow everyone I danced with (believe it?). I danced with Lincoln, Duane, Dale, Errol, Bob, Mark, Dee, and John. I had more fun than I have had for a long while, and my feet hurt more than they have for a long while. I'm about too tired to go to bed. Tomorrow I will have to get up and get ready for our class trip before 9:00.

April 18th, 1953 - Dear Diary, today is a day to remember. I went to Jacob Lake and the Colorado Bridge on a class party.

Dear Diary, now I'm really tired! Mr. Christensen called for me about 9:00, and we (our class) met at Orderville before starting on our trip. I had never been past Fredonia, so I felt excited when we started on the trip. At the Fredonia sawmill just out of town, Mr. Christensen showed us around and took us through the sawmill. Never have I seen so much desert and "wide open spaces" or such a change as we drove up the steep winding road to the Kaibab, where the beautiful pine trees grew in thick forests. My, but they were pretty. I sat back and looked and looked some more. That is the kind of country I just love.

Criminy! There was a change as we came around a curve and House Rock Valley came into view. Oh, so many feet below us, beneath the bright vermilion cliffs with its hazy range of mountain in the background. We stopped at the sawmill. This flat valley seemed endless as we sped across the sand. Mr. Christensen pointed out the gorge that formed the Colorado River. I was really expecting something. Finally, we saw the big white bridge and everybody jumped out.

I ran to the rock wall and looked off. It didn't seem deep enough. I thought it was at least ½ mile down and that mighty river was so very big. I thought it would look like a ribbon. When I went to the bridge and looked down and heard the rocks we threw hit the water, I decided it was deep. After eating a lunch and waiting for the boys who tried to get to the river to come back, we drove back to Jacob Lake and passed the lodge and café where Mama and Daddy had lived for a few months and where Wendy had been born because of the big snow storm.

We drove to the lake. I liked the lake and also the snow we found sheltered under the eaves of an old barn. We played ball on the flat guarded by a huge pine. The air was so sweet and the wind rustled through the trees. I felt as if I wanted to stay on the Kaibab for weeks. Mama had told me so much about Jacob Lake and the time she spent out there. After we ate a supper, we drove up to the café for a minute, and I looked around and tried to imagine how it looked 16 years ago. We were in a hurry to get home, so we said goodbye to Jacob Lake and turned homeward as the sun was slipping through the pines.

For souvenirs, I have a chunk of bark from House Rock, a pretty shaped stone from Colorado Bridge, and a pine bough from Jacob Lake.

April 19th, 1953 - Dear Diary, it has been a nice Sunday, but I am still tired from yesterday.

April 20th, 1953 - Dear Diary, I am to sing again on Wednesday in a band concert at Kanab and Fredonia. It seems I'm always singing.

April 21st, 1953 - Dear Diary, in school we had a show, "Spirit of Stanford." I didn't get to M.I.A. Daddy had the car.

April 22nd, 1953 - Dear Diary, I guess the song was all right, but I didn't sing loud enough, and in one place I forgot it.

April 23rd, 1953 - Dear Diary, it seems this has been a long week. Maybe I just have Spring Fever. It is so nice out-of-doors.

April 24th, 1953 - Dear Diary, my head has been aching all day. I feel so tired and cross. Maybe I am getting scarlet fever.

April 25th, 1953 - Dear Diary, I haven't done much today. I cleaned the front room and got $6 mixed with the trash and burned it.

April 26th, 1953 - Dear Diary, I was afraid I was not going to conference, but luckily I got to. Mr. Peterson talked. He is just wonderful.

April 28th, 1953 - Dear Diary, Daddy was going to Kanab on business, so Wendy, Ikie, Mama, and I went to "The Greatest Show on Earth."

April 29th, 1953 - Dear Diary, I am to sing "Mother Machree" in a Sunday program the 10th. Honest! I'm tired of singing, and I don't seem to have the time to practice any more. I don't know if I'll ever learn "The Kiss."

May 1st, 1953 - Well! Dear Diary, tonight was the Junior Prom. Wendy had a date, Lincoln was at Logan, and I went alone. I didn't have any fun, but I know who did. Different from last year, huh?

May 2nd, 1953 - Dear Diary, I am tired today. I guess it is from sitting on the bench last night.

May 3rd, 1953 - Dear Diary, did I tell you that on Friday a famous violin player played for us? He was a foreigner and played on a very famous violin.

May 4th, 1953 - Dear Diary, Lincoln, Wendy, and I went to dance practice. It was lots of fun.

May 5th, 1953 - Dear Diary, in place of M.I.A., they had the Stake Dance Festival at Kanab. We went.

May 6th, 1953 - Dear Diary, for the first time in weeks, I had a music lesson. I'm getting tired of music lately (that's all I think about).

May 7th, 1953 - Dear Diary, to pay for a lesson, I tended kids and cleaned house for Stocking's at 25 cents an hour.

May 8th, 1953 - Dear Diary, we saw a show, "The Elephant Boy." Tomorrow we are going to go to the Region Dance Festival.

May 9th, 1953 - Dear Diary, my, I'm tired. Today we had the Dance Festival at Dixie Sun Bowl. There were hundreds of people. I had a big day.

Dear Diary, this morning we woke up to snow, and it's the 9th of May, and of all days the day for the big dance festival. Luckily, when we reached Dixie, it was windy and cold but not snowing.

We practiced from 1:00 to about 3:00. Oh, there were hundreds of kids.

I went to Grandmas. I met Mavis and Janis, Cora, Lincoln, and Gary and others from Enoch. The Sun Bowl was all lit up, and the seats were crowded. The dancing with hundreds of others was wonderful, and so was watching the other dancers, but I was tired when we finally got home.

May 10th, 1953 - Dear Diary, I sang the song, but for the 3rd time in a song, I blundered the 2nd verse. I don't know what is the matter.

May 11th, 1953 - Dear Diary, I am tired of singing! But I know I shouldn't feel that way. Mama says not to.

May 12th, 1953 - Dear Diary, I worked at Stocking's again, and stayed down to Lincoln and Bessie's farewell dance.

May 13th, 1953 - Dear Diary, today I wonder if it is worth what I go to for my lessons. He doesn't teach me much for a $1.00.

May 14th, 1953 - Dear Diary, in school we selected next year's officers. Wendy is yearbook editor. In F.H.A., I was chosen song leader.

May 15th, 1953 - Dear Diary, I am reading my last book for this year, Jessie Sturte's "The Thread that Runs So True." It's really something.

May 16th, 1953 - Dear Diary, last night was the post prom, but I didn't have any reason to go. Today we had a party for Sam!

May 18th, 1953 - Dear Diary, we got the yearbooks today.

May 19th, 1953 - Dear Diary, today was a band and chorus concert. After school, I helped Stocking's.

May 20th, 1953 - Dear Diary, tonight was the grade school play, "Molly Be Jolly." I surely liked it.

May 21st, 1953 - Dear Diary, well so long to the Seniors. They had a wonderful graduation, but it will seem so different, Lincoln being out of school. We had Daddy's watch fixed and prepared for a present. It was a sad night. Most of the graduates cried or felt mighty solemn and so did some of the others. Afterwards they had a dance.

May 22nd, 1953 - Dear Diary, school is out after today, and I know I will enjoy summer.

May 23rd, 1953 - Dear Diary, Lincoln and Sammy went to the ranch (who could stop them), and Wendy went to work (in a café). So it seems a bit different, but I'm going to be busy, so I will have no time to worry. Today I helped Stocking's move. I don't know why, but I feel I am glad they will be gone for a while (I'm ornery).

May 26th, 1953 - Dear Diary, tonight was Mia Maids' rose tying. It was nice. We wore formals.

May 27th, 1953 - Dear Diary, I'm occupied with chasing the dog, cats, and chickens off my flower beds.

May 28th, 1953 - Dear Diary, raising flowers around here is a job. I wonder if I will ever have any.

May 29th, 1953 - Dear Diary, the folks from Glendale have been up to see us, so Neldon can help fix the truck.

May 30th, 1953 - Dear Diary, Grandpa and Aunt Becca came to see us. The boys and Wendy came home Sunday.

May 31st, 1953 - Dear Diary, I am having more darn trouble with my flowers. The dog insists on laying on them. I transplanted some Monday, and today I planted some more, but they are so frail and small. I doubt if they will grow.

June 2nd, 1953 - Dear Diary, I worked in Kanab at house cleaning for Burgoyne's.

June 3rd, 1953 - Dear Diary, today I worked in Kanab for Burgoyne's. She certainly pays for my work, $1.00 an hour.

June 4th, 1953 - Dear Diary, we had an outdoor party and roast for Daddy's birthday. He is 46.

June 5th, 1953 - Dear Diary, I haven't been a bit lonesome, even with the kids gone (I have plenty to do).

June 6th, 1953 - Dear Diary, today was the opening of fishing season, and my, what a day!

June 7th, 1953 - Dear Diary, I went to Sunday school and Testimony meeting today. Ikie was made a deacon.

June 8th, 1953 - Dear Diary, I worked at Kanab again. I have learned to like all of them and have enjoyed working there.

June 9th, 1953 - Dear Diary, I am having quite a time trying to get my flowers to grow and in convincing the dog to keep off.

June 10th, 1953 - Dear Diary, there are some people renting the house at Hidden Lake. I helped them clean house. Their names are Bill and Elaine. They are a young couple and have a little boy (Brian).

June 12th, 1953 - Dear Diary, there is certainly a lot to be done, and I haven't started 4-H yet. I don't seem to get a chance.

June 13th, 1953 - Dear Diary, I am so busy. I hardly have time to get lonesome, and Lincoln says I'm getting fatter (oh dear).

June 14th, 1953 - Dear Diary, Jeremy and Elton are here. It has been quite a day. I came to St. George with Marion to help Grandma.

June 15th, 1953 - Dear Diary, I met the next door neighbors. Mary (14) took me swimming (she is a corker), loves toast and ice water.

June 16th, 1953 - Dear Diary, I help get meals, do dishes, clean house, and iron. Marion and Valoyce's baby is very cute. They are sure proud of him. Grandpa took me to a show, "Yanks Ahoy," and a western show (double feature).

June 17th, 1953 - Dear Diary, Mary introduces me to a lot of kids. She is always phoning and planning something, like eating in the park or playing tennis or going up town to see a show, "I thought we were skating." She wants me to keep my glasses off, because I have eyes like the movie stars (she says).

June 20th, 1953 - Dear Diary, I saw "Small Town Girl." I have enjoyed myself here, and I hope I have helped. St. George is a nice place. I saw Delynn, Virine, and the baby. We went uptown (I spent all my money, about $4.50).

June 21st, 1953 - Dear Diary, I came home (by way of Duck Creek) with Steven and Dores. I would have liked to stay longer, but Mama needs me.

June 22nd, 1953 - Dear Diary, everything is in a mess and guess who came? Aunt Lorraine and Jay and the kids. Everyone is so glad to see each other.

June 23rd, 1953 - Dear Diary, we all went fishing in Bary Canyon, then all came here, and we had a supper and get-together. I stayed at LeAnn's for M.I.A.

June 24th, 1953 - Dear Diary, today I cut the taller grass around the lawn. Jay and Lorraine stayed at Orderville.

June 25th, 1953 - Dear Diary, Jay is sick, so they went home today. They didn't even stop to say goodbye or get their things.

June 26th, 1953 - Dear Diary, I am at my flowers again. I wish they would grow. Elton and Jeremy went home with Arvilla and Lawrence, when they went up to Salt Lake to Fred and Marie's wedding.

Dear Diary, Mr. Stocking is back. I can't figure it out. I feel I could scream whenever I think of singing. I never (hardly ever) practice, and I seem to forget how to carry a tune. I don't know why, and I should not say this, but I hate to see him come back. It cripes me. Why should I feel this way?

July 1st, 1953 - Dear Diary, Cram's boy Roger is staying with us.

July 4th, 1953 - Dear Diary, we went to the ranch today and had lunch with Bullocks. It was nice, and I felt I didn't want to come home, but they say the ranch, now, is "no place for a girl," and the boys don't welcome me there, but it is my ranch as well as theirs. I don't understand.

July 6th, 1953 - Dear Diary, it seems all there is to do around here is work, and that can surely get tiresome.

July 7th, 1953 - Dear Diary, today it rained. It seemed so good. It has been so hot. I went to Lydie's Canyon tonight.

July 8th, 1953 - Dear Diary, I am trying to set out more flowers and start a rug. I am wondering if I will get my 4-H.

July 9th, 1953 - Dear Diary, I went to town today with Wendy to 4-H. We decided on going on the mountain the 16th.

July 11th, 1953 - Dear Diary, we all (except Daddy and Ikie) went to the show, "The Greatest Show on Earth." It was very good.

July 12th, 1953 - Dear Diary, I stayed downtown about all day getting things rounded up for our 4-H trip.

July 13th, 1953 - Dear Diary, tonight a large flood washed down the canyon. My, but it was big!

July 15th, 1953 - Dear Diary, we came to Duck Creek at about 3:00 this evening. We chose camp #35 and set up our tents.

July 16th, 1953 - Dear Diary, it has been a wonderful day, even if it has rained a lot. We put on our skit tonight, "Three Little Pigs."

July 17th, 1953 - Dear Diary, we have met a few new people and had our troubles with neighbors and wet wood and paper (fire building).

July 18th, 1953 - Dear Diary, we hated to leave so soon, but the prospects of warm and soft beds and dry living quarters makes us more anxious to be home.

July 19th, 1953 - Dear Diary, already I am missing the fun we had at Duck Creek. I went to Sunday School.

July 20th, 1953 - Dear Diary, I have found it rained down here as well as up to Duck Creek. There was quite a flood in Lydie's.

July 21st, 1953 - Dear Diary, Kenneth is staying at LeAnn's and at the ranch. We don't see much of him.

July 22nd, 1953 - Dear Diary, Roger is still staying with us. We all go up Lydie's Canyon, and the other night we had a party.

July 23rd, 1953 - Dear Diary, there is plenty of work, but I still seem to have something missing. Maybe it's spare time.

July 24th, 1953 - Dear Diary, it has been quite a day. I stayed down town about all day, then we came to the fireworks and the dance (I stayed at Rita's).

July 25th, 1953 - Dear Diary, I didn't get home until afternoon, so I had to hurry and get my work done so I could go to the scout jamboree.

July 26th, 1953 - Dear Diary, today has been an eventful day: the signing of a Korean truce and the driving out of the polygamists of Arizona.

July 27th, 1953 - Dear Diary, I sewed today on my 4-H shoe bag. It is finished (after all my troubles).

July 28th, 1953 - Dear Diary, this year is certainly different from last year. This summer with three gone, most of the time it gets lonesome, and there is so much work to help with. I never seem to be able to really "live." I mean think about writing, drawing, and climbing the hills. I really enjoy roaming by myself and taking some paper and pencil along. This summer, I have hardly left the house. I also have 4-H sewing to do, and oh criminy, you know how I do sewing.

August 2nd, 1953 - Dear Diary, today was fast Sunday, and we all went to meeting. Roy and Allison's baby was blessed and named.

August 3rd, 1953 - Dear Diary, I know I should feel thankful for where and how I live. Have you heard about it?

August 4th, 1953 - Dear Diary, I went to an M.I.A. dance for once and finally after all of my troubles.

August 5th, 1953 - Dear Diary, I have been finishing some sewing and ironing today, and Mama told me some of her past stories.

August 6th, 1953 - Dear Diary, today was Wendy's day off. Annette is here, so all of us girls had a get-together at the Y.

August 8th, 1953 - Dear Diary, Lincoln and Annette and Wendy and Mark went to Kanab tonight. It sure made me feel lonesome. I wanted to go, but you know how things are, and I had to stay home.

August 9th, 1953 - Dear Diary, I helped Wendy with her Sunday school class this morning. Karen and Ora May and Sherman are staying up here a few days.

August 10th, 1953 - Dear Diary, it isn't quite so lonesome with the girls here. They sure find lots to do and lots to get into.

August 11th, 1953 - Dear Diary, there isn't much to write about. All we do is work. We entertain ourselves (me and Mama) by discussing Wendy and Roger (King Fish) Fisher. He goes with her, but she prefers someone else. Guess who? Of course (Mark).

August 13th, 1953 - Dear Diary, last night Lincoln and Sam came from the ranch. The girls bought marshmallows, and we had a party (it was lots of fun).

August 14th, 1953 - Dear Diary, Thursday (13th) Neldon and Eva came home. They brought the table. It was Aunt Becca's mother's table.

August 15th, 1953 - Dear Diary, Mama, Ikie, Lincoln, Sammy, and me went to "Red Mountain," a show. We are all worried about the future. Daddy wants to sell the ranch. He thinks Lincoln cannot go to school (Cedar) unless we do.

August 17th, 1953 - Dear Diary, we bottled peaches today and (as usual) prepared dinner for (menfolk). That seems to take all day. Jeremy Easton is helping with the hay.

August 18th, 1953 - Dear Diary, Daddy wants to sell the ranch. He thinks it is the only way out if Lincoln goes to school. We all dislike the idea, but maybe it is best that way.

August 19th, 1953 - Dear Diary, I have been doing a lot of sewing lately for the fair. Tonight we went up Lydie's with the menfolk. We gathered gum.

August 20th, 1953 - Dear Diary, Wendy and I went to 4-H today at Orderville.

August 21st, 1953 - Dear Diary, this afternoon I went to Aunt Eva's and got my buttonholes made and the seams on my dress pinked. I have sewn some more and helped iron.

August 22nd, 1953 - Dear Diary, I finished my pajamas today and cleaned house. Mama and Daddy went to conference, and I tended kids.

August 23rd, 1953 - Dear Diary, I went to Kanab to conference. Mr. Peterson talked about being true to the faith (it was wonderful).

August 24th, 1953 - Dear Diary, we bottled peaches today, and I made a skirt from a dress. I went to a 4-H party at Madeline's.

August 25th, 1953 - Dear Diary, today I tended kids while all of the folks went to Kanab. I bottled 17 quarts of beans meanwhile (oh criminy).

August 26th, 1953 - Dear Diary, today I have been bottling beets (I got tired of beans). I bottled six quarts.

August 27th, 1953 - Dear Diary, I have ironed my 4-H things so they will be ready to be entered in the morning.

August 28th, 1953 - Dear Diary, I entered my articles today. Here's hoping? Mama went to Logan. I left the kids with Daddy and went to the dance.

August 29th, 1953 - Dear Diary, my, what a day! Guess what ribbons I got. One on slip, one on flowers, one on pajamas, one on book, two on dress, two on beets, two on peaches, two on flowers, three on shoe bag, three on beans. I felt pretty good when I saw so many pretty ribbons. I know I tried!

I guess I shall bring up that name again. It happened this way: Early this morning, at about 9:00, while I was in the middle of the work of getting ready for the fair (Lincoln had gone down earlier and said he would be back for us in a while), Ikie and Sam came running in saying, "Cathy, Nathan and Gerald are out there for us." Well, they had to wait for us, and they seemed to be in a hurry.

Mike and Mary Ann's shoes disappeared, and I didn't know what Mike would wear for pants. I raced around and had to wonder at Lincoln (he must have been busy). I remembered Roger had to have new shoes, so I sent them down (with Ikie) to get them. Now maybe I could get the kids ready, if I knew they were not out there waiting.

Luckily, we were ready when they came back. I wondered how things would go. We all went out to the car. Nathan was at the wheel. Gerald was by him. All the kids got in the back, then Gerald decided to too. Well, Ikie held the door open and told me to get in (the front), so we did (I was holding Mary Ann). Ikie finally got in, and we started off.

I'll never know how Nathan liked this arrangement. The car looked quite a sight, and he had quite a hard time getting it to manipulate (you see it's a crate). I didn't feel quite as stupid as I thought I would. I could talk a little. I don't know why the change.

Maybe because I felt the situation was different and maybe just because.

When we got there, they jumped out in a hurry. I don't blame them. They ran up the sidewalk. I looked at the exhibits and waited around until noon, then we came home with Lincoln this time. I stayed home 'til 7:30 then went to the talent show. Then Rita, Ester, and I went to "David and Bathsheba." I had had enough sitting on the bench the night before. We haven't gotten the entries out of the fair yet. I hope we get them! All and all, quite a day!

August 30th, 1953 - Dear Diary, they all made it to church. Under my supervision, it is a bit harder.

August 31st, 1953 - Dear Diary, Mama finally! I was glad she could go, and I was glad when she came home.

September 1st, 1953 - Dear Diary, we have been sewing today, and I have caught up on a bit of drawing "for the summer."

September 2nd, 1953 - Dear Diary, I made a cake for Mama's birthday. I drew her two pictures of Mary Ann and Michael.

September 3rd, 1953 - Dear Diary, today we have been sewing for school.

September 4th, 1953 - Dear Diary, still sewing.

September 5th, 1953 - Dear Diary, I have cleaned house all day and am so tired.

September 6th, 1953 - Dear Diary, I helped in Wendy's class. In meeting I bore my testimony on the "Book of Mormon."

September 7th, 1953 - Dear Diary, it has been quite an eventful day. Logan and Natalie, V and R, and we all went to Bryce and Pine Lake to fish and celebrate.

September 8th, 1953 - Dear Diary, it is time to say goodbye to "summer days." School started today.

September 9th, 1953 - Dear Diary, we have one new teacher and need a new music teacher. Mr. Stocking left for Idaho.

September 10th, 1953 - Dear Diary, I hope I can make a success of this year. I go in planning that I can be what I want, but soon find out there are the same problems as the year before. I went to the dance tonight and spent a horrible time. I'm certainly not going to the next dance.

September 12th, 1953 - Dear Diary, I worked today (as usual). Wendy is at Salt Lake to the State Fair.

September 13th, 1953 - Dear Diary, Mama and I taught Wendy's class today.

September 14th, 1953 - Dear Diary, Lincoln is at Cedar to college. Doesn't it seem different?

September 15th, 1953 - Dear Diary, we have two new teachers: Mr. Avinney and Miss Crawford (music). I am taking chorus.

September 16th, 1953 - Dear Diary, I am to sing Tuesday, so I have to go back to practicing again.

September 17th, 1953 - Dear Diary, school seems much the same as it ever was. The books are certainly going to cost! $3.15.

September 18th, 1953 - Dear Diary, I have an awful cold, and am I glad this is the last of this week.

September 19th, 1953 - Dear Diary, I cleaned house a little, but I sure feel sick with this cold I have.

September 20th, 1953 - Dear Diary, I stayed home today. If I go to Logan Friday, I had better get better. I read in "The Book of Mormon."

September 21st, 1953 - Dear Diary, I didn't go to school today. It seemed about like summer again, just Mama, Mike, and Mary Ann and me.

September 22nd, 1953 - Dear Diary, I am to sing next week (I'm glad it isn't this week). I went to school and M.I.A. today.

September 23rd, 1953 - Dear Diary, I am so glad. I get to go to Logan for F.H.A. (I am song leader). I am worried about money. We haven't any.

September 24th, 1953 - Dear Diary, I came home from school and have been busy getting ready all evening. I'm so excited!! Four of us are going.

September 25th, 1953 - Dear Diary, what a day. We left home at 6:00 and got there at Logan by 2:00. We went downtown, shopped, and went to a show.

September 26th, 1953 - Dear Diary, we went to meetings from 9:00 to 4:00. At 7:00, we went to a football game with New Mexico. I had a wonderful day.

September 27th, 1953 - Dear Diary, we went to two meetings this morning. We left to come home at 2:00 and got home after midnight.
    Dear Diary, we had a wonderful trip to Logan. I was so glad I could go. Glennia, Georgia, Joy, Donna, and I went up with Mr. Quinney and his family (I certainly like them). It was a long ride, but I enjoyed it. Oh, but Logan is beautiful! I just love it. The campus was just perfect, I thought. We stayed in the Rural Arts build-

ing. Friday we visited Aunt Lorraine and Uncle Jay. We went to a show and rode in a taxi. We didn't get to bed until after 12:00. We were locked out.

Glennia really showed us a good time Saturday (she was very nice). We went to meetings in the new Union building. It was grand. That night we went to a football game. Sunday morning, we went to a sunrise meeting and to College Institute. I really enjoyed those meetings. We ate all of our meals in the college cafeteria. We played we were in college and some thought we were. Sunday, after the car was fixed, we left for home. We were all tired and glad to be going home. I was in debt $1.50. I took only $5.00. We reached home after midnight. What a wonderful time!

September 28th, 1953 - Dear Diary, you can bet I'm tired today. I'll always remember that trip. I surely like Logan. I hope I go there again.

September 29th, 1953 - Dear Diary, I sang tonight in M.I.A. "Live Life in a Sweet Key." I sang it about as well as I hoped I would, but I still need to improve.

September 30th, 1953 - Dear Diary, I am having trouble getting my school books. I haven't enough money. I am still not as friendly as I should be.

October 1st, 1953 - Dear Diary, I am glad I am not a Freshie this year. They are really getting the works.

October 2nd, 1953 - Dear Diary, the Freshie Frolic was tonight. I didn't go because I just simply had no reason to go.

October 3rd, 1953 - Dear Diary, I cleaned house today, and Roger, Mike, and I went up Minche Canyon and gathered armfuls of red, yellow, and brown leaves.

October 4th, 1953 - Dear Diary, we wrote a family letter to Lincoln. Everyone wished him a happy birthday. I wish we could have seen him.

October 5th, 1953 - Dear Diary, we Sophomore girls, after going to the Seminary party at the Muddy, went to Kanab to the show "Call me Madam." At 1:00, we had a big supper.

October 6th, 1953 - Dear Diary, we girls are tired this morning. Tonight most of us are going to the Stake play of Book of Mormon Days, "Them also I must bring."

October 7th, 1953 - Dear Diary, tonight we had the F.H.A. sleeping party. My, was it fun! Listen, and I will tell you about it. I was on the committee to make the spook alley for the Freshie initiation, so I stayed down after school. We made pans, then hurried to the dump in Ora May's car to find springs and a box. Rita and I rode on the front of the car to hold the box on. Jeaneete and Georgia got on the front with us, and we had quite a time keeping on.

We asked Jeremy, Lavoy, and Bernale to go to the Cave with us and find some bones. They consented, and away we went. What bones they found!! Horse heads and vertebrae!! At school, we set up the spook alley. They went through elevator on hands and knees (they were blindfolded and had shoes off). They fell into coffin and crawled through bones to the underground tunnel. They cross the railroad, each rung had something wet and grimy on it. They entered the devil's den. Each step was covered with wet grass. At the landing was a snake and cobwebs. They stepped into a pan of cold, green water and spaghetti (worms). The devil met them and while it thundered, gave them an F.H.A. hand. They climbed the back entrance and were led back into the gym where they were treated to candy chews with chili peppers.

At about 10:00, we put on our pajamas, made our beds on the gym floor, and started pillow fighting. After we had the fights, there was a game ending in a program. Rita and I told "The Three Billy Goats." We ate afterwards and went to bed at 3:30.

October 8th, 1953 - Dear Diary, I am quite tired today. I am cleaning up our room. Mary Ann has moved in with us girls.

October 9th, 1953 - Dear Diary, we Sophomores had our class party tonight up Main Canyon. It was quite a time. We ate five gallons of chili.

October 10th, 1953 - Dear Diary, the leaves are certainly beautiful now. I did the usual Saturday cleaning.

October 11th, 1953 - Dear Diary, church was very good today. Gary talked in both meetings. He certainly gave good talks.

October 12th, 1953 - Dear Diary, tonight was to be the F.H.A. ceremony, but we couldn't go because of transportation.

October 13th, 1953 - Dear Diary, in M.I.A. we had a Mia Maid and Mother party. Mama and I both gave talks.

October 14th, 1953 - Dear Diary, I broke my glasses today. It certainly made me feel terrible. We were in such a mess anyway (maybe I just won't get any again).

October 15th, 1953 - Dear Diary, we are having tests in Seminary and Biology. I got the highest in the class in Biology, 95 ½%.

October 16th, 1953 -Dear Diary, last night was the Deer Hunter's Ball. It was a good dance "for some." Today in school everyone was dead tired.

October 17th, 1953 - Dear Diary, I ironed today and cleaned house. At least somebody has an eventful life. Wendy went with Roger, again.

My Dearest Diary

October 18th, 1953 - Dear Diary, I went to my class in Sunday school. I went to meeting and fireside afterwards at Janet's.

October 19th, 1953 - Dear Diary, it is certainly getting cold weather. I am reading "Toward the Morning."

October 20th, 1953 - Dear Diary, we went to M.I.A. tonight. Our lesson was on the sacrament.

October 21st, 1953 - Dear Diary, I met Uncle Harold, Grandpa Jackson's brother.

October 22nd, 1953 - Dear Diary, we woke up to snow this morning. It seems like winter. Daddy is at the ranch.

October 23rd, 1953 - Dear Diary, we had home evening tonight, eight of us. I wrote a letter to Lincoln. We sure miss him at times like this.

October 24th, 1953 - Dear Diary, I picked up walnuts today. We have quite a few, but I could find only one bucketful of apples.

October 25th, 1953 - Dear Diary, Daddy wasn't home and the car wouldn't go, so Wendy and I walked to Glendale to Sunday school. It was nice.

October 26th, 1953 - Dear Diary, I got four A's, one A-, and one B+ in my grades for the term. I will have to improve in Home Ec. and P. E. and keep the others.

October 27th, 1953 - Dear Diary, I didn't get to go to M.I.A., and I sure feel mad about it. Daddy had the car, so we just couldn't go.

October 28th, 1953 - Dear Diary, we had a party dinner for Mike. It doesn't seem like he is five years old already.

October 29th, 1953 - Dear Diary, we are having quite cold weather now. It feels about like winter.

October 30th, 1953 - Dear Diary, Wendy and I are dressing as Raggedy Ann and Andy. I'm making our masks.

October 31st, 1953 - Dear Diary, I went to Kanab today to order glasses! I was afraid I wouldn't get to.

November 1st, 1953 - Dear Diary, today was Testimony Meeting. Gary and Cora came over from Enoch. They went to meeting.

November 4th, 1953 - Dear Diary, I am busy making signs for our Sophomore skit. We are having a time; we have too many disagreements. I cleaned house for Rust's today after school.

November 6th, 1953 - Dear Diary, I think I will get my glasses soon (thank goodness).

November 7th, 1953 - Dear Diary, I helped Eva tonight.

November 8th, 1953 - Dear Diary, I went to conference today! Three meetings. It was wonderful. Bishop Barry and Mr. Clark were there.

November 9th, 1953 - Dear Diary, I have my new glasses. I quite like them. They are different.

November 10th, 1953 - Dear Diary, we went to M.I.A., and just as we left Orderville the car gave way. We packed water from the creek in ½ pint tin cans. We had a time.

November 11th, 1953 - Dear Diary, the 13th is Sadie Hawkins Day dance. I sang "I Believe" in an assembly, accompanied by clarinets.

My Dearest Diary

November 12th, 1953 - Dear Diary, I was hoping I could ask Dale or Jeremy but Rita's date fell through and only she has a car, so I'm out of luck.

November 13th, 1953 - Dear Diary, my, what a dance! I can't say how many I danced with, but I know I danced all but two sets, and am I tired.

The Sadie Hawkins Day dance was really fun! Now I can have something to console me, as I sit on the bench. I can remember I danced "then."

Arlene and I really had a time. I danced with Sharon Lamb on the boy's choice. I danced with about a dozen different guys and only one twice, Dale. I had to keep up with Arlene and that darned RaNell.

November 14th, 1953 - Dear Diary, Leana and Todd came today and stayed all night. Roger came to see us again. Virginia and him must have had a fight.

November 15th, 1953 - Dear Diary, the car is still broken down. Wendy and I caught a ride with Uncle Logan this morning. I went to meeting and fireside too.

November 16th, 1953 - Dear Diary, I finished my story, "Cranberries for Thanksgiving," tonight.

November 17th, 1953 - Dear Diary, the car is broken down still. My, a plight!

November 18th, 1953 - Dear Diary, we mighty Sophomores are having our dance the 21st. Wish us success.

November 19th, 1953 - Dear Diary, "The Chimers" presented a program today. I was asked to sing "When Irish Eyes Are Smiling" to their accompaniment. Three of us did.

November 20th, 1953 - Dear Diary, we saw the show "Bird of Paradise" in school today. It was certainly sad; everyone cried. It was a tragedy.

November 21st, 1953 - Dear Diary, we had our dance. I didn't dance much, many did. We had a big crowd and cleared $50.60. The theme was "you, you, you."

November 22nd, 1953 - Dear Diary, because I had such a cold, I stayed home today. A missionary, "Jacobs," came to talk to us. He stayed all day.

November 23rd, 1953 - Dear Diary, I stayed home today. I am reading "Rose in Bloom." It is about the very best book I have ever read. I am making a rag doll too. So I have plenty to do, while I recover from this cold. I had a miserable time at the dance.

November 25th, 1953 - Dear Diary, I went to school today. We had an assembly and dance. Lincoln came home tonight. I am telling you, we were mighty glad to see him again.

November 26th, 1953 - Dear Diary, we had a wonderful Thanksgiving. We three went to the dance and really had fun. Anyway I did, for a change. I danced five times.

November 27th, 1953 - Dear Diary, I haven't done much today. I drew and finished reading my book. It seems good to have a holiday.

November 28th, 1953 - Dear Diary, I went to another dance. We are having enough for one weekend, don't you think?

November 29th, 1953 - Dear Diary, I went to church twice today. I still have my cold. I was supposed to sing tonight.

November 30th, 1953 - Dear Diary, it is surely getting cold now days. It will soon be real winter.

December 1st, 1953 - Dear Diary, here it is December all ready. Before long it will be Christmas.

December 2nd, 1953 - Dear Diary, I didn't get to M.I.A. again. It was pretty cold, and Daddy said I couldn't go, even if I was having a class (just dancing).

December 3rd, 1953 - Dear Diary, I am making doll clothes for the ward bazaar. I stayed after school tonight to practice our song for the band concert.

December 6th, 1953 - Dear Diary, I went to two meetings today.

December 8th, 1953 - Dear Diary, we are all (band and chorus) practicing for the concert. We girls have a sixtet.

December 9th, 1953 - Dear Diary, the concert was tonight. The chorus sang "Out Where the West Begins," "Comin' Through the Rye," "I'll See You Again," and "It's a Grand Night for Singing."

December 11th, 1953 - Dear Diary, there was a game and dance tonight. Valley beat Escalante, but the referees cheated. It was an awful game. The dance was a bad one too. I'm as dumb as I was two years ago. I wonder if I won't ever grow up and act the way I should. I've got to learn how to be more friendly.

December 15th, 1953 - Dear Diary, in M.I.A. tonight there was a program about Christmas and a story-play.

December 16th, 1953 - Dear Diary, I stayed with Rita tonight. We went to a show and to the Valley and Fredonia ballgame. We won.

December 18th, 1953 - Dear Diary, Mama and Mary Ann and me went down to Orvillia's and made Christmas candy.

December 19th, 1953 - Dear Diary, we cleaned house today and sent off Christmas packages.

December 20th, 1953 - Dear Diary, we all went to Sunday school and meeting today. Eva and family came up, and we made candy.

December 21st, 1953 - Dear Diary, we haven't been having much school these days. We practice too much for the pageant. Did I tell you I have the solo part in "O Holy Night?" It's hard, but if I practice enough, I should be able to do it.

December 23rd, 1953 - Dear Diary, today in school we had an assembly and dance. It was quite fun. We had the pageant tonight and, oh dear, I didn't do very well.

December 24th, 1953 - Dear Diary, we are going to have a wonderful Christmas. Everybody is home and, I think, happy. We have been getting ready all day.

December 25th, 1953 - Dear Diary, we have had a nice Christmas, even if there isn't any snow. We three went to the dance tonight.

December 26th, 1953 - Dear Diary, I stayed home tonight and tended the kids while Mama and Daddy went to the show. Wendy was with Mark.

December 27th, 1953 - Dear Diary, Lincoln talked in meeting tonight. Wendy and I went to fireside at Madeline's. Mr. LeFever talked about his life experiences.

December 28th, 1953 - Dear Diary, I can find plenty to do. I have a good book, the piano to play, two new songs to learn, and an oil paint set.

December 29th, 1953 - Dear Diary, today is Wendy's birthday. A bunch of girls planned a surprise party. She had a date with Mark, so there was a lot of arranging to do. We kept it pretty much a secret until the time for it. It was at Jeanette's. Mark took her down at about 7:30. We were having a family party at home. Eva and Orvillia and families came up, and we had cake and ice cream. Lincoln and I were a bit late for Wendy's party, but we made it. It was very nice. About 2 dozen were there. Everyone had a lot of fun, I think. Anyway, I know I did.

December 30th, 1953 - Dear Diary, it seems good to be having holidays. Wendy has a date about every night. We have lots of fun.

December 31st, 1953 - Dear Diary, it doesn't seem like 1954 is so near. I hope it brings what we all need.

1954

January 1st, 1954 - Dear Diary, I have gone to two dances, last night and tonight both. These nights have really been fun.

January 2nd, 1954 - Dear Diary, tonight was the Seniors' dance. Don't tell anybody, but I only danced with Lincoln. I wonder if I'll ever dance more.

January 3rd, 1954 - Dear Diary, today I cleaned house and mopped floors. I'm rather tired.

January 4th, 1954 - Dear Diary, we started school today. Lincoln went back to Cedar. Well, here goes for a new year.

January 5th, 1954 - Dear Diary, I stayed to help Mrs. LeFever tonight after school, then I went to M.I.A.

January 6th, 1954 - Dear Diary, I get a chance to sing in the Festival, if I can get a song. I don't know about "The Kiss" Mr. Stocking got for me. I am probably not up to it, Miss Crawford says, but she is going to give me a chance.

January 8th, 1954 - Dear Diary, I went to a dance tonight. There was not much of a crowd. Rita and I enjoyed our books (in the dressing room). You see I'm still pretty silly at times.

January 9th, 1954 - Dear Diary, we kids went to the show "Plymouth Adventure" tonight. We took Karen and Ora May.

January 10th, 1954 - Dear Diary, I have tended kids about all day. Tonight four of us went to meeting.

January 11th, 1954 - Dear Diary, it's getting to be like spring. We have had no snow since early December.

January 12th, 1954 - Dear Diary, I stayed after school tonight and had my second lesson on the piano. I'm working for the play.

January 13th, 1954 - Dear Diary, I went to Miss Crawford's tonight. She is going to help me! She is a very sweet and talented person.

January 14th, 1954 - Dear Diary, tonight Mama and I went to singing Mothers and Daughters practice. I'm really getting my music this week.

January 15th, 1954 - Dear Diary, Valley is playing at Hurricane tonight. The bus is running. I want to go, but there is no chance.

January 16th, 1954 - Dear Diary, Mama, Daddy, and I went to Kanab today. I'm afraid Mama is sick. I got a coat for my birthday.

January 17th, 1954 - Dear Diary, we have all gone to church again today. I tended the kids this afternoon.

January 18th, 1954 - Dear Diary, I guess we will really have winter after all. It is really beginning to snow!

January 19th, 1954 - Dear Diary, we surely had fun in M.I.A. tonight. The Explorers gave the Mia Maids a party. Goodbye 15th year.

January 20th, 1954 - Dear Diary, I can hardly believe I'm 16. It seems I should really be a grown young lady, but I really don't feel very different.

January 21st, 1954 - Dear Diary, I am going to try to learn "I Love Thee" for the Solo-Ensemble. Do you think I will be a success?

January 22nd, 1954 - Dear Diary, we had a game with Cedar. They won the excitingly close game by seven points.

January 23rd, 1954 - Dear Diary, Mama, Wendy, and I went to Mavis and Robert's reception tonight at Cedar. We saw Lincoln. We left at 5:00, stayed till 11:00, got home at 2:30.

January 24th, 1954 - Dear Diary, Aunt Orvilla is at Cedar, so I stayed down with LeAnn tonight. Mary Alice and Lloyd have a baby girl.

January 25th, 1954 - Dear Diary, because the electricity was off, we didn't go to school till 1:00 today. Chad, LeAnn, and I caught up on our rest.

January 26th, 1954 - Dear Diary, in school we have been getting our pictures taken. I stayed at LeFever's and went to M.I.A.

February 1st, 1954 - Dear Diary, I went to Kanab tonight to practice for the Relief Society pageant. It lasted for hours.

February 2nd, 1954 - Dear Diary, the M.I.A. speech festival was held tonight in Kanab. Most of the M.I.A. went. It was good.

February 3rd, 1954 - Dear Diary, I have a lot of practicing to do on "I Love Thee" before the Solo-Ensemble.

February 4th, 1954 - Dear Diary, I practiced in the Mothers and Daughters chorus tonight. Only two Sophomores were there.

February 5th, 1954 - Dear Diary, it seems good to stay home and read tonight and not have any place to go.

February 6th, 1954 - Dear Diary, I cleaned house today, and tonight I tended Karen and Ora May and Sherman.

February 7th, 1954 - Dear Diary, it was conference and the pageant today at Kanab. It has all been wonderful.

February 8th, 1954 - Dear Diary, I have been quite awful today. The Sophomore class sluffed Seminary. We didn't go in the building.

February 9th, 1954 - Dear Diary, because of what we did yesterday, we have to write a 1,000 word theme and lose 10% from our grades.

February 10th, 1954 - Dear Diary, I've been reading "Foxes of Harrow." It is not very good. I don't advise young people to read it.

February 14th, 1954 - Dear Diary, I went to church today, and tonight I gave a short talk on prayer. I went to fireside at Georgia's.

February 15th, 1954 - Dear Diary, I am trying to learn "I Love Thee" for March 10th. I don't know if I shall ever learn to count time.

February 16th, 1954 - Dear Diary, I had a lesson at LeFever's tonight. I don't know if I am earning them or not. I cause too much trouble.

February 17th, 1954 - Dear Diary, we had a game with Hurricane tonight. We were beat again. The team cannot cooperate. Jeremy G. and Wane R. try to play the games by themselves. They think the other players don't know how. It's quite aggravating! There are four or five Sophomores on the team. If they could get a good enough chance, we could win more often.

February 20th, 1954 - Dear Diary, Wendy and I stayed with the kids while Mama and Daddy went to St. George temple.

February 21st, 1954 - Dear Diary, we all went to meeting and Sunday school today.

February 22nd, 1954 - Dear Diary, we got a holiday today. This morning I went on the hill. This afternoon we practiced. We also went to the auction for M.I.A.

February 23rd, 1954 - Dear Diary, tonight in M.I.A. the Mia Maids put on the skit "The Three Little Pigs." I was the wolf.

February 24th, 1954 - Dear Diary, I didn't practice again. The assembly practicing is all I have time for.

February 25th, 1954 - Dear Diary, the assembly we have been planning for a month is tomorrow. We have been practicing in the gym.

February 26th, 1954 - Dear Diary, it has really been a day!! First the assembly, then the game and the dance at Kanab.
Dear Diary, we had our chorus assembly today. It was a story of gypsies. We all dressed in costumes. RaNell and I did a dance and sang a song, "Merry Zingerellas."

The game with Kanab was quite an experience. The first quarter Jeremy E. went out on fouls, but all through the game we led or we were tied. It was very close. The last two minutes we were one point ahead. Kanab got a foul shot, and we were even. The game was all but over when suddenly Kanab got a basket. They beat us by two points. We were mighty disappointed.

February 27th, 1954 - Dear Diary, tonight we beat Cedar! In the last game of the season to be played home at Valley. I sure wanted to go, but I stayed home again.

February 28th, 1954 - Dear Diary, today has been a good Saturday. I don't know why, maybe it is just the thought that tomorrow is March.

March 1st, 1954 - Dear Diary, it doesn't seem like March already. The 10th will soon be here, and I don't know my song yet.

March 2nd, 1954 - Dear Diary, I stayed at LeFever's again. It seems like it has been a month since last week. I went to the road show.

March 3rd, 1954 - Dear Diary, I practiced with Amy tonight, and I have a lot of practicing to do yet. I tended Sherman tonight.

March 4th, 1954 - Dear Diary, I have the darndest luck! I've caught a cold and am hoarse. I won't get to practice until I'm better.

March 5th, 1954 - Dear Diary, tonight was the last basketball game, and I had to stay home. When I was told what happened, I'm glad I did.

Dear Diary, I stayed home from the last game tonight. I wanted to go, but I have a cold that I must get over, so I went to bed. I thought we could win the game with Enterprise, so we would not be the last in the division. I heard there was to be a party afterwards for the ball boys and their dates. Rita and I heard Jeremy,

My Dearest Diary

Errol, and some of the other boys telling about some kinds of plans, and we wondered.

We never could have guessed, Dear Diary, what they really had in mind. I was really shocked!! Wendy told me Jeremy, Duane, Von, and Charles were drunk! I can hardly feature it. Jeremy just wouldn't do that, I thought. Wendy and Ikie were disappointed too. I haven't seen him yet, but I think he is sorry, or will be sorry. We were beat again. It was a hard game, but that is no excuse for getting drunk!

March 6th, 1954 - Dear Diary, we had a party for Mary Ann today on her 3rd birthday. My cold is worse today, I hope I get over it soon.

March 7th, 1954 - Dear Diary, I stayed home today and tried to get over my cold. If I have it by Tuesday, I can't go to Delta.

March 8th, 1954 - Dear Diary, I'm trying to practice my song, even if I'm not quite over my cold. Tomorrow I have to sing.

March 9th, 1954 - Dear Diary, today we had an assembly and at noon started to Delta. We went on the bus with Kanab. We got there at about 7:00.

Dear Diary, this morning we gave an assembly, had lunch, then left for Delta. Kanab went with us. It was not as bad as we thought it would be. When we reached Delta at about 7:00 we were met by different people who took us to homes where we were to stay. Amy S., RaNell, Rita, Varue, and I stayed at a Bishop Bazil's home. We were treated wonderfully! That night we went to a play and a dance. We also had a party.

March 10th, 1954 - Dear Diary, what a day! The Solo and Ensemble. It certainly has been wonderful and very educational! We met some very nice people too.

Today was really a day. We listened to many numbers and enjoyed them. After lunch, we gave our parts. I thought I would be terribly scared, but it wasn't half as bad as I thought. Guess who was the judge? Ned Wright. He was simply wonderful. He made us all feel so good. He talked to us all individually. It certainly meant a lot to all of us.

We will soon find out how we rated and why. The Solo-Ensemble was really a thrilling experience, but everyone was pretty tired when we reached home after midnight. I think I will always remember March 10th, 1954 as a grand experience!

March 11th, 1954 - Dear Diary, we ten who went to Delta are surely tired this morning. We are drawing names for the girls' day dance, for fun!

March 12th, 1954 - Dear Diary, I drew Norman Martin's name. I wonder if I will dare ask him to go with me to the dance.

March 13th, 1954 - Dear Diary, today I cleaned house as usual. I finished "Pilgrim's Inn." I really liked this book.

March 14th, 1954 - Dear Diary, it seems good to have us all home again. We all went to church together today.

March 15th, 1954 - Dear Diary, I am on the committee to plan for two parties (one to Las Vegas). I doubt if we can go.

March 16th, 1954 - Dear Diary, I stayed at LeFever's tonight and went to M.I.A.

March 17th, 1954 - Dear Diary, we are all planning for the carnival Friday.

March 18th, 1954 - Dear Diary, we saw a show, "The Lion and the Horse," today. 9th and 10th P.E. classes danced today. I danced with Duane, Jeremy, and Steven.

March 19th, 1954 - Dear Diary, tonight was the big night. There was a crowd. I danced with Lincoln and Mark. Jeremy won a prize (a lantern).

March 20th, 1954 - Dear Diary, Lincoln, Mama, and I went to the Gold and Green Ball in Kanab. It was too crowded to be much fun.

March 21st, 1954 - Dear Diary, church was good today. I went to fireside after meeting. We saw films on ancient American ruins.

Dear Diary, I don't know if I'll ever know why Jeremy got drunk, but I believe he won't do it again. How could a person drink 12 cans of beer? I am glad I did not see him drunk. It's hard to understand Jeremy. I think he is a bit confused himself. I wish I could help him. He reminds me of myself sometimes.

I hope he doesn't harm his mind and body by his actions. Jeremy has a wonderful physique (body). He is 6 ft. 1 in. and very athletic. He is quite shy and self-conscious, but I believe he can someday make a very manly man if he can be strong enough and resist temptations that would harm him.

March 23rd, 1954 - Dear Diary, in M.I.A. tonight we had a party with the Explorers at Roy's. It is snowing again.

March 24th, 1954 - Dear Diary, tonight was the F.F.A. banquet. I didn't get to help because it was storming too bad to go to town.

March 25th, 1954 - Dear Diary, Daddy is taking Mr. LeFever's place for two days. Some of the F.F.A. boys and he went to Salt Lake.

March 26th, 1954 - Dear Diary, tonight we stayed home. Usually we go someplace on Friday nights.

March 27th, 1954 - Dear Diary, it is beginning to seem like spring. It is hard to stay indoors and clean house.

March 28th, 1954 - Dear Diary, I gave the scripture in meeting tonight.

March 29th, 1954 - Dear Diary, in school we Sophomores are planning for our assembly.

March 30th, 1954 - Dear Diary, in M.I.A. we had a Mothers and Daughters stake meeting. It was wonderful! Mrs. Frost talked to us about honoring womanhood.

March 31st, 1954 - Dear Diary, I'm having a hard time asking Norman to the dance. He really evades and stays out of school.

April 1st, 1954 - Dear Diary, although we haven't played any bad pranks, it has been a pretty good April Fool's today.

April 2nd, 1954 - Dear Diary, it has been quite a day today. Our assembly turned out all right, much to our amazement, but the F.F.A. dance wasn't so good.

April 3rd, 1954 - Dear Diary, tonight we kids went to the show "Lure of the Wilderness." We surely liked it.

April 4th, 1954 - Dear Diary, we had a party for Rodger today. Grandpa and Aunt Becca came to see us this afternoon. We all went to church.

April 5th, 1954 - Dear Diary, today is Monday. Wednesday is Girls' Day! I asked Norman for that date. Guess what he said? The dear boy has to go to the herd.

April 6th, 1954 - Dear Diary, I stayed down to M.I.A. tonight. We had chorus practice afterward. We are trying to learn songs for the stake festival.

April 7th, 1954 - Dear Diary, what a day and night! We haven't had much school today. We had assemblies (programs) instead, and what a dance! I sang "Pretend."

Dear Diary, Girls' Day has been quite a time. Now about the dance! You know I drew Norman's name. When I asked him yesterday, he told me he wouldn't be here. Well, today he came as usual. He didn't have to go to the herd after all. He didn't tell me. I found out another way. When I got home, Mama told me I had better ask Norman again since there was a change in plans. I wouldn't consider it, but finally with Wendy's and Mama's darings, I decided I would (just for fun and suspense). Wendy drove me down to his house, and after finally finding the gate, I went to the house. There were two doors, and as I was going to one, somebody appeared at the other.

"Looking for somebody?" Norman was standing there.

"Since you are not to the herd, will you go to the dance with me?" I asked.

Norman answered, "I think we are having a class party tonight."

I told him I thought all of the Senior girls were going to the dance, and the boys were not any place around. We argued for a while. I thought it was quite fun! We came to the agreement that if he had not gone to the party by 9:00, I would take him to the dance. I felt pretty sure I had my date. Daddy had to go to town and muddle up our plans. He didn't get home until 9:30. We were pretty sure to go by that time.

We hurried to Norman's but alas! Every light in the house was turned out and the door was locked. If other excuses fall through, Norman can rely on a bed. Don't believe this ruined the night for me; I had a wonderful time. I just wish the dance would have lasted longer. I danced with Jeremy once. I didn't get to dance with Dale or Ted.

April 8th, 1954 - Dear Diary, it has been a tired day for most everyone. It's bad to have a dance on a weeknight.

April 9th, 1954 - Dear Diary, we all stayed home for once on a Friday, believe it or not.

April 10th, 1954 - Dear Diary, I stayed home all day, as usual. Wendy went with Lynn James (Jeremy's big brother) to the ball at Cedar.

April 11th, 1954 - Dear Diary, I have been to three meetings today. I sang in the Mothers and Daughters chorus tonight in meeting.

April 12th, 1954 - Dear Diary, "The Robe" is at Cedar and we have been hoping to see it. Mr. Christensen promised us Sophomores we could go.

April 13th, 1954 - Dear Diary, I stayed down to M.I.A. tonight. Afterwards, we had singing practice. Lincoln, Lynn James, and Mr. Quinney are the only boys.

April 14th, 1954 - Dear Diary, we Sophomores have been playing baseball again. We have some mighty boy players!

April 15th, 1954 - Dear Diary, 14 of us went to Cedar to "The Robe." It cost us two dollars, but it was worth it.

April 16th, 1954 - Dear Diary, we saw another show "Golden Girl" today, and the Juniors gave their assembly.

April 19th, 1954 - Dear Diary, we Sophomores gave the Freshman a party out on the sand dunes. My! What a time!
    Dear Diary, what a party we just had! I'm not saying this with a smile either, but maybe I should. It wasn't really bad, but Jeremy really does shock me! First one way, then another. Oh, I guess it wasn't all his fault. He's not the shy boy one might think he is, not when some not-so-shy girls flirt around. Too many find him too attractive. Those 9th grade girls (but not LeAnn this time) love to craft love. What can a poor boy do when four or five pick on him

but enjoy himself? Jeremy knows how to pull girls down sand dunes, and hide shoes, and chase girls. Those girls and he aggravate me!

Then going home, those girls and boys must have walked home (from Carmel). There was a full moon also. Maybe I judge too harshly, but do you blame me? Dale is not so, maybe you would say, extreme as Jeremy. He is more tempered or controlled, I believe. Jeremy, Duane, Marlynn, and those girls rode in the back end of the truck. Dale, Errol, Al, and us kids rode in the front end of the truck. We sang and had a good time.

April 20th, 1954 - Dear Diary, everyone is tired today. I feel as if I had been through a war.

April 21st, 1954 - Dear Diary, in M.I.A. yesterday, I sang "I Love Thee." We finally had the music festival.

April 22nd, 1954 - Dear Diary, the pipeline broke today, so school was out at noon. I climbed to the top of the mountain.

April 23rd, 1954 - Dear Diary, this four leaf clover I found should have brought me luck. I'm afraid it didn't, but the prom was nice.

April 24th, 1954 - Dear Diary, we haven't done much today but discuss last night.

Dear Diary, our class sure seems to like to play ball. While we were playing in Seminary, I found a four leaf clover. However, it didn't bring much luck for the dance (Junior Prom). I had a date with Lincoln (Wendy was with Lynn). The floorshow dance was very pretty. Jeremy helped dance, and boy! He looked nice, suit jacket and all. He was quite self-conscious, but he sure was handsome. I didn't do much dancing. I'm glad Wendy had a good time at her dance, and I'm glad there was a crowd. The gym was really decorated. The theme was "Hawaiian Memories."

Today, Nathan asked me about that certain corsage. He wondered if it were dusty.

April 25th, 1954 - Dear Diary, I went to conference this afternoon. Spencer Kimball was the authority. He gave some wonderful talks. I sang in the stake chorus.

April 26th, 1954 - Dear Diary, I heard Jeremy say he wants a date for Friday. He can surely be surprising. I wonder!!

April 27th, 1954 - Dear Diary, the high school went to Zion National Park today. Rita, Jenny (a new rival), and I went down with Mr. LeFever. It was a fun day. We went to weeping rock. Tonight was rose tying in M.I.A. We had a wonderful meeting.

April 28th, 1954 - Dear Diary, I worry and wonder! Gosh, I'd like a date for Friday. Here is hoping I get a chance!

April 29th, 1954 - Dear Diary, I believe the dates were called off. Maybe they couldn't make up their minds about who to ask.

April 30th, 1954 - Dear Diary, I went to the dance with Lincoln. Jenny and Nathan went together. It wasn't much of a dance for me, but Jenny did get a dance from Jeremy!

May 1st, 1954 - Dear Diary, in despondent moods, writing poetry surely helps! I have written "Future Promise."

May 2nd, 1954 - Dear Diary, Grandma is here with us to stay for a while. She came late Friday night. We had good meetings today.

May 3rd, 1954 - Dear Diary, it seems like time is passing too fast. It certainly is like summer.

May 4th, 1954 - Dear Diary we went over to the dance festival in Kanab, tonight for M.I.A.

May 5th, 1954 - Dear Diary, we are about through with our studies for the year. It seems good.

May 6th, 1954 - Dear Diary, with such spring in the air everybody is inclined to recline on the lawn or play ball.

May 7th, 1954 - Dear Diary, we, in chorus, are getting tired of "Lebrastrume," and the changing keys we sing it in, but Jim is a good director.

May 8th, 1954 - Dear Diary, Wendy went with Lynn to the band festival in St. George. Next year's F.F.A. officers are at Logan. We voted for student officers.

May 9th, 1954 - Dear Diary, we all went to church for Mother's Day. Wendy bought a card and slip for Mama yesterday.

May 10th, 1954 - Dear Diary, I know Mama is sick, and I can't seem to do anything about it. Even though she was sick, she went to our chorus concert.

May 11th, 1954 - Dear Diary, we were vaccinated today. The yearbooks came. After M.I.A. I practiced a song. I rode home with Lynn and Wendy.

Dear Diary, I went with Rita to type during Home Ec. I was sitting in the window watching a ballgame and looking at a magazine when Nathan came in the room. He came up to me and said, "Want something?" After wondering a while, I said I did. He hands me a furry dangling monkey he had found.

May 12th, 1954 - Dear Diary, "12th of May, Sophomore Day." We girls won two games this morning. The boys won games this afternoon. We have been to two classes today.

May 13th, 1954 - Dear Diary, we don't seem to be having much school lately. We do what we want in chorus and read in English.

May 14th, 1954 - Dear Diary, today we had V day. We didn't work much. Tonight, we all had a party on the flat. It was some party!

May 15th, 1954 - Dear Diary, I went to town today. I have a job at "Fern's." Goody! I am going to try to learn songs so I can go to June conference.

May 16th, 1954 - Dear Diary, I thought I was supposed to sing tonight, but I'll be glad to wait. It was the Aaronic Priesthood's night.

May 17th, 1954 - Dear Diary, it really does not seem like this could possibly be the last Monday of school, although it is green and very much like summer.

May 18th, 1954 - Dear Diary, I have been asked to go to 4-H camp in Cedar Monday. We are also having a camp at Zion that week.

May 19th, 1954 - Dear Diary, the Seniors had their closing assembly today. It will be different without them. It still hardly seems possible they were Seniors.

May 20th, 1954 - Dear Diary, school was held a half of the day because of the band's going to Kanab races. Eva stayed here until they had their party.

May 21st, 1954 - Dear Diary, many dreams are going with these Seniors. Maybe you understand how disappointed I am.

To Jeremy

As I sit beneath the roses filled with rainy dew,
Jeremy, I am thinking of you.
I am remembering what has just past.
It seems the year has gone all too fast.

My Dearest Diary

This year has meant a lot to me,
And to you. Don't you agree?
Little things, but things precious to my memory.
A blush, a smile, a sweet feeling, action reveling.

Jeremy, sometimes spring sunshine
Is like this of yours and mine.
Spring is wonderful and new, our feelings are too.
Something yet in bud,
But oh, what will the future bring
Blossom or frozen sting?

May 22nd, 1954 - Dear Diary, I worked for Mrs. Young today, and boy am I tired!

Dear Diary, it certainly does not seem possible for it to be the year it is. Along with some of these Seniors go many of my dreams. Don't you remember how I dreamed about operettas, dates, and all? Things will go on, but they will seem so different. But what am I talking about? Didn't I decide I don't like him? And didn't I decide most Seniors are ornery?

May 23rd, 1954 - Dear Diary, in meeting we got two new councilors. Mr. LeFever and Alfred Crofts are leaving us. I sang "The Lord's Prayer."

May 24th, 1954 - Dear Diary, I worked in the garden today. Wendy is at Zion. I also cleaned house.

May 25th, 1954 - Dear Diary, I wrote two poems today. I went to town with Wendy. We went to M.I.A. Lincoln is a counselor.

We Are Youth

We are youth, you and I,
And we want to know

Now, not by and by.
What will help us to grow?

We want to be free.
We want to be strong.
Now, to be worthy.
What will keep us from wrong?

We are youth, you and I,
And we will know
It is the noble truth
That will help us to grow.

The truth makes us free.
Abide in its strength.
Now, we will be worthy,
For life an eternal length.

A Reason for Things

I climbed the mountain today and sat in a tree.
From that branchy nest
I beheld near and far away
Scenes of now and scenes to be.

I thought how things are planned and why they are so.
For each God given thing,
There is a reason for His hand;
A meaning for things that grow.

I understood then why I stated I would go,
When Father God said to us
On the day earth He created,
"Go now and worthiness show."

I think He must have known we would miss Him.

My Dearest Diary

So to help us remember
He gave tokens of love to show
The ways to keep us from sin.

I would say these gifts of love are the trees,
Also the bright flowers, grains,
The golden sunshine from above,
The songs of birds and bees.

As I descended the mountain and homeward turned,
I felt thankful for His blessings,
Springing from a pure fountain
To supply earth hearts that yearned.

May 26th, 1954 - Dear Diary, Grandpa and Aunt Becca came today for a while. I have been working on my "Treasure of Truth" book and drawing.

May 27th, 1954 - Dear Diary, I went to town tonight to practice those songs. I waited while Daddy went ward teaching.

May 28th, 1954 - Dear Diary, I got my hair cut today and a permanent. I wrote another poem, "A Symbol," and read from my "Treasure of Truth."

A Symbol

I think of you as a golden promise
With the cleanness of truth.
To me you are a symbol of noble growing youth.

You represent to me one ideal,
Of advancing young manhood.
For one like you one day, I will true love reveal.

To you also one will surely come,

Whom you can rightly admire.
Then you too will achieve your eternal desire.

To this fulfill, do that which
You have learned to know
Will help you in both body and spirit to grow.

May 29th, 1954 - Dear Diary, I've been cleaning house today. We thought Mike was lost. The men folk were late at the chores. I sprained my ankle.

May 30th, 1954 - Dear Diary, my ankle surely hurts. I feel quite silly limping around. Deloy Easton talked to us in fireside. It was very good.

May 31st, 1954 - Dear Diary, we went to the graveyard and decorated graves. We saw Mary Alice, Lloyd, the baby, and Jay and Adery.

June 1st, 1954 - Dear Diary, the M.I.A. had a party tonight up Main Canyon. It was quite fun. But guess who is at New Castle for I don't know how long?

June 2nd, 1954 - Dear Diary, today I cleaned house. I found a new way to make varnish. I tended kids and cooked about all day long.

June 3rd, 1954 - Dear Diary, what a time! A bunch of us kids had a party for Lincoln L. C., Lynn J. E., and Deloy E. at Zion Park. Gosh, but it was a lot of fun.

June 4th, 1954 - Dear Diary, the family had a party for Daddy tonight up Lydie's Canyon. All four reservoirs are surely pretty. We have five!

June 5th, 1954 - Dear Diary, Wendy went to Logan for Girl's State this morning.

June 6th, 1954 - Dear Diary, I stayed at Rita's today so I could go to the Award Meeting in Kanab tonight.

June 7th, 1954 - Dear Diary, I practiced at Mrs. Young's tonight. Going to Salt Lake and singing in the tabernacle will sure be thrilling.

Dear Diary, with all of these parties I have been to, I should not feel lonesome, but I don't get to see everybody. Everybody doesn't go. Brother's teasing doesn't help either. It seems like school has been out for a month or so. In a way, things are like last year. It is interesting when Wendy has a boyfriend. Now it is Lynn, Jeremy's big brother.

June 8th, 1954 - Dear Diary, I wrote another poem today. In M.I.A. we were graduated to the Jr. Gleaner class.

June 9th, 1954 - Dear Diary, all day I have been getting ready to go to Salt Lake. Money is quite a problem!

June 10th, 1954 - Dear Diary, well, we made it. We got in Salt Lake about 6:00 p.m. and had our first practice in the Barret Hall Tabernacle.

June 12th, 1954 - Dear Diary, today we practiced at 4:00 p.m. We certainly have wonderful directors, Loraine Bowman, Crawford Gates, Elvis Terry, and George Cannon. Our practices are long and tiring. We get very tired, but they are very wonderful. Can you imagine how thrilling it would be singing with 1,600 others? 88 stakes were represented, with some awfully sweet boys and girls. There were a number of different states represented. I talked to Francis Webster. I saw Lorren and said hello to Gary. It seemed so good to see them.

Tonight I saw part of the M.I.A. dance festival. It was certainly beautiful. Adding this to the general session and its grandness fulfilled a day I had long dreamed of. The 12th of June I hope will remain forever in my mind where I might remember its wonderfulness. I can only partly tell of its blessings to me. I have never experienced such a day in all my life! From 4:00 p.m. to 11:00 p.m. we sang for thousands. At 7:00 p.m. we were on radio's "The Church of the Air." We gave three programs.

Sunday, to completely fill our thrilled emotions, we attended two meeting with the general authorities in charge. Again, we sang in a choir for the general conference. When our president and prophet of the church told us he had never known such accomplishment of youth, we felt nothing this side of heaven could possibly be so truly wonderful. I say "we" because I feel not just mine, but hundreds of other testimonies were strengthened.

Dear Diary, this has been a day to treasure forever. We presented our chorus of 1,600. May its memory help me in my growth.

June 13th, 1954 - Dear Diary, after attending two general meetings, we left Salt Lake and our many new friends to travel until we reached home at 12:00 p.m.

June 14th, 1954 - Dear Diary, tonight we had quite a party at Mama, Classira, Lorraine, Eva, and Orvilla's ranch out on the Muddy. It is good to all be together again.

June 15th, 1954 - Dear Diary, tonight we went to M.I.A. and saw films on first aid and safety. We need to know first aid after last night's mishap.

June 16th, 1954 - Dear Diary, those boys are surely aggravating. Why on earth can't Duane learn how to grow up and help, not hinder, others? I am glad for Jeremy's not being in town where he might easily cut his hair like an Indian too and shave off all his hair but a strip across his head.

My Dearest Diary

June 18th, 1954 - Dear Diary, yesterday Mama and her sisters went to St. George, and I stayed and tried to cook and run the house. It seems like everyone is sick because of it.

June 19th, 1954 - Dear Diary, we sure had a heck of a Sunday school class! But meeting was very good. Mr. D. Wayne Rose talked.

June 20th, 1954 - Dear Diary, I'm a bit mixed up. Today is Sunday. Yesterday was Saturday. Pardon me.

June 21st, 1954 - Dear Diary, I worked at the café today for the first time. What a time I had! I'm tired.

June 22nd, 1954 - Dear Diary, that party we were going to have didn't seem very hopeful, so some of us went to Kanab to the show "Red Garters." It was quite corny.

June 23rd, 1954 - Dear Diary, what an experience I have had today at older girls' and boys' club camp. I'll tell you about it.

Dear Diary, I went to Red Canyon today for older girls' and boys' club camp with Mr. Rose, Carolyn L., Norma B., Jaketta W., and Charles P. It was really a wonderful experience. I met a lot of nice people and had lots of fun.

Three boys from foreign countries were there. Two were 4-H exchange students from Pakistan, India. One was a government agriculture man from Iran. They were certainly interesting to talk to. We all got together and played a game, danced, and learned about 4-H club camp planning. Jaketta is to be mayor at club camp (I voted for her). Wayne Jones is to be secretary (I nominated him). Marba Wilson is to be reporter. Carolyn and I are both on committees. From this trip, I have learned more about 4-H and what it means to be a member. We really have some fine leaders! I think Mr. Rose is wonderful. And I thank him that I got this privilege to attend the 4-H camp.

June 24th, 1954 - Dear Diary, tonight (until 6:00), I washed dishes at the Y. It was Janet's day off.

June 25th, 1954 - Dear Diary, there was a dance tonight at Glendale for LaRee and Dick, but I didn't go. Just because.

June 26th, 1954 - Dear Diary, we all went fishing today up Main Canyon. Boy did we get wet, but it was fun picnicking in the rain.

June 27th, 1954 - Dear Diary, guess who came home? He didn't come to Sunday school though. It seemed good to see him at meeting.

June 28th, 1954 - Dear Diary, I washed dishes yesterday for a while, and today I was a waitress for the second time. Sometimes it is a worry.

June 29th, 1954 - Dear Diary, I took Wendy's place today from 1:30 to 9:30. It wasn't too fast, and Virginia was there to help me, thank goodness.

Dear Diary, it really seems good to see Jeremy again (though from a distance). I don't know exactly when he came home, but he was in town Thursday, the 24th. Rita told me he didn't come to Sunday school. I wonder why. I saw a glimpse of him at meeting. Today when Wendy took me to work, we met two guys headed toward Orderville. I recognized Steven, but it took me a minute to realize the other one was Jeremy. He had a huge hat on.

Later, Wendy picked them up on her way home (I knew she would). They had been to Kanab working on the new school building. Every morning at 3:00 a.m. (they said), they went to Kanab to work. Afterwards, they hitch hiked home. What do you think of that? You just never know what those two are going to do next! But pretty good for them (I hope?). Jeremy wondered if I was working on Wendy's day off. Wendy told him. He wondered if we were going to stay at the Y this summer. I wonder if he really wanted to know, and if so why? Well, as I said before, you just never can tell?

June 30th, 1954 - Dear Diary, I didn't work today. Michael, Mary Ann, and I went for a swim in the creek. Then we all went to Lydie's Canyon.

July 1st, 1954 - Dear Diary, I worked in the kitchen from 1:30 to 9:30. It certainly doesn't seem like it is July already.

July 2nd, 1954 - Dear Diary, as I said before "you never can tell about those two boys." Working in Kanab? Like heck! They are working for Jack (making bricks).

July 3rd, 1954 - Dear Diary, the electricity went off today at the Y, and we had quite a time. Although Steven and Jeremy are at the Y, I have not seen them.

July 4th, 1954 - Dear Diary, I got to go to Sunday school today but had to work this afternoon. It is too bad, but Jeremy doesn't come in the café.

July 5th, 1954 - Dear Diary, I'm so darn tired, but I went to the dance anyway. It was worth it. I danced with Lincoln, Paul, Donald, Mark, and Lee.

July 6th, 1954 - Dear Diary, we didn't have a very busy day today at the Y. At least those two dare sit on the café porch, and while I was in the midst of mopping.

July 7th, 1954 - Dear Diary, today I had a day off. It has gone by fast. I got some clothes ready for tomorrow, cleaned house some, and went swimming.

July 8th, 1954 - Dear Diary, I am trying to learn to drive. But after what happened today, I don't believe I can get another chance (under these conditions).

July 9th, 1954 - Dear Diary, we haven't had much business at the Y lately, but we have had a few fun but silly times. Fern is gone for a while.

July 10th, 1954 - Dear Diary, I am terribly tired tonight. My legs, feet, and ankle really ache. I feel as if I could sleep 40 hours. Lena and Curtis are here for a while.

July 11th, 1954 - Dear Diary, Jeremy finally came to Sunday school again. At work today, I made two $.75 tips and one $.35. A lucky day.

July 12th, 1954 - Dear Diary, I worked again today. I bought a necklace and earring set made from copper flake. Lena and Curtis are here.

July 13th, 1954 - Dear Diary, I met a boy at the café today. His name is Alfred. He is from L.A., California. He said he would write to me.

July 14th, 1954 - Dear Diary, at the café we can eat only $.75 worth. Mama's Sunday school class girls had a swimming and sleeping party here.

July 15th, 1954 - Dear Diary, I worked in the kitchen for Janet's day off.

July 16th, 1954 - Dear Diary, today has been my hardest day at the Y. I had a few hours alone. I took the front. Virginia sure is a help.

July 17th, 1954 - Dear Diary, today was the Cornellia reunion, Grandpa Thomas's 100th birthday. We really have seen a lot of folks.

July 18th, 1954 - Dear Diary, I went home to Sunday school this morning. It was a day off, so I got to go to meeting. J. Adury gave talks. I finished reading "The Book of Mormon."

July 19th, 1954 - Dear Diary, it seems good to have days off. I made an apron today for 4-H.

July 20th, 1954 - Dear Diary, well, I'm working again. I doubt if I will ever finish the book I am starting, "Gone with the Wind."

July 21st, 1954 - Dear Diary, it is good to have a few hours to do as you please once in a while. The orchard is loaded with apples and shade.

July 22nd, 1954 - Dear Diary, it is a different kind of summer this year isn't it!

July 23rd, 1954 - Dear Diary, I worked today with Wendy. I made $2.20 in tips.

July 24th, 1954 - Dear Diary, I have been in town about all day (and night) for the 24th. I helped Mama then went to a show and a dance.

July 25th, 1954 - Dear Diary, I thought I would have a "real" Sunday today, for a change, but I didn't get to any church at all. I took Janet's place.

July 26th, 1954 - Dear Diary, we (Rita and Evelyn) are at Duck Creek 4-H camp. It rained today. There was a meeting and skits tonight, and what a hard bed!

July 27th, 1954 - Dear Diary, just think! I'm an officer. I introduced the skits and talents tonight. I sang a song for a talent.

July 28th, 1954 - Dear Diary, it is too bad we have to break camp so soon. We got home just this afternoon. I am really sun burned and tired!

July 29th, 1954 - Dear Diary, my, I am glad I don't have to work out front. My face is really sore, but this 4-H camping is really worth it.

July 30th, 1954 - Dear Diary, I worked in the kitchen today.

July 31th, 1954 - Dear Diary, it is about time we had a Saturday to clean up!

August 1st, 1954 - Dear Diary, I went to church today and stayed down after meeting at Rita's. I practiced with Mrs. Young. Jeremy went back to New Castle again.

August 2nd, 1954 - Dear Diary, I was a waitress today. It certainly is hard getting "into it" again. I got my paycheck.

August 3rd, 1954 - Dear Diary, we were planning on going to Cedar today, but Daddy's plans fell through, so Wendy and I went shopping anyway.

August 4th, 1954 - Dear Diary, Grandpa and Aunt Becca came today. I have gone to town 2 or 3 times today. It has been raining.

August 5th, 1954 - Dear Diary, I worked in the kitchen today. In a way I am getting lonesome for school. Maybe I'm just lonesome.

August 6th, 1954 - Dear Diary, I worked out front again. This morning I sewed on a 4-H dress. Being a waitress can be quite nice.

August 7th, 1954 - Dear Diary, today was a busy day for the Y. I got me another pair of shoes (white moccasins).

August 8th, 1954 - Dear Diary, because I worked middle shift today, I got to go to meeting tonight.

August 9th, 1954 - Dear Diary, I worked in the kitchen today. Tonight, I tended the kids while Mama and Daddy went to a party.

August 10th, 1954 - Dear Diary, Wendy and Dad and I went to Cedar with Garn today. Isn't it fun and easy to spend money?

August 11th, 1954 - Dear Diary, sometimes I get so darn anxious for school to start. I'm tired of working in a café, and I'm lonesome.

August 12th, 1954 - Dear Diary, I love days off! I hope I can get my 4-H sewing done before the fair. I want to sing in the talent contest too.

August 13th, 1954 - Dear Diary, Friday the 13th is an unlucky day. Janet got sick, and I covered her day off. But a party in Lydie's Canyon was fun tonight.

August 14th, 1954 - Dear Diary, tonight Mama and I went to the show "Young Bess." It was very good.

August 15th, 1954 - Dear Diary, I got to go to church today. I felt lucky! I worked for Wendy for a few hours.

August 16th, 1954 - Dear Diary, I finished my 4-H dress today. I have been sewing all day.

August 17th, 1954 - Dear Diary, I worked today. It is tiring but not as bad as it was.

August 18th, 1954 - Dear Diary, it certainly was a busy day at the Y today.

August 19th, 1954 - Dear Diary, I didn't work today at the Y. Mama went to Salt Lake for the Jackson reunion.

August 20th, 1954 - Dear Diary, the Jehovah Witnesses are at the Y. They cause enough trouble. Religion is really getting discussed.

August 21st, 1954 - Dear Diary, I worked in the kitchen for Janet today. I miss Mama and the kids.

August 22nd, 1954 - Dear Diary, we had a wonderful conference today and fireside tonight. I sang "The Lord's Prayer." Marlyn spoke to us. It was held at Wendell's father's home.

August 23rd, 1954 - Dear Diary, guess what?! Roy wants me to sing over the radio K.S.U.B. in Cedar City.

August 24th, 1954 - Dear Diary, so we went to Cedar today. Making a radio recording was quite an experience!

August 25th, 1954 - Dear Diary, the voice on the radio today didn't sound much like mine. I hope I can do better at the contest.

August 26th, 1954 - Dear Diary, these last few days have been rush, rush. I wonder if I will get my 4-H things done after all. I am so tired of working. I will be glad when school starts.

August 27th, 1954 - Dear Diary, thank goodness we closed early tonight, so I got to see Wendy give her talent and win 1st attendant to Miss Kane County. Oh, it was wonderful! We were so proud!

August 28th, 1954 - Dear Diary, I sang "My Friend" in the talent contest tonight. I didn't win. I didn't expect to, but it was quite an experience to remember and profit by.

August 29th, 1954 - Dear Diary, Wendy and Lynn, Deloy and Norvel, Jeremy and Joy, and Donna are all going to Grand Canyon tomorrow. Don't I always get the hard deal?

August 30th, 1954 - Dear Diary, it must have been a nice trip for all who went. I don't know when I will ever learn to completely control my feelings.

August 31st, 1954 - Dear Diary, wouldn't it be nice to go to Grand Canyon! They had a good trip today, Wendy says.

September 1st, 1954 - Dear Diary, there was another Easton party tonight. Lynn is going to Massachusetts for maybe 2 years. I went to a 4-H party instead. It was a lot of fun.

September 2nd, 1954 - Dear Diary, I am getting a bad cold, and boy I feel miserable. Mark was hurt quite seriously in a car wreck. We all feel very sorry.

September 3rd, 1954 - Dear Diary, I have an awful cold tonight. It is quite aggravating. I wonder if it is mostly emotional!

September 4th, 1954 - Dear Diary, Mama said I am still too sick to work at the Y, so Wendy worked for me toda, while I tried to lose this cold.

September 5th, 1954 - Dear Diary, oh, how I am hating to go to work again. Today was very busy, but I helped everyone.

September 6th, 1954 - Dear Diary, isn't it mean to have to work up until the day school starts!! Boy, and am I glad it is.

September 7th, 1954 - Dear Diary, today was the first day of school. It really seems good to be going back. We have two new teachers.

September 8th, 1954 - Dear Diary, I have to miss Chorus and Type again for algebra! But I have to get it. It was a good school day!

September 9th, 1954 - Dear Diary, when I went to the music (conducting) class in Kanab, I went with Jim to see Mark. He is quite sick. That was a bad wreck.

September 10th, 1954 - Dear Diary, the music class is quite nice. Mr. R. C. is our teacher. He is a wonderful teacher.

September 11th, 1954 - Dear Diary, I wrote Mark a letter. I don't know what he will think, but I know he needed one.

September 12th, 1954 - Dear Diary, for the last two days it has really been raining! I went to church twice today.

September 13th, 1954 - Dear Diary, in History, our assigned seats were: Steven, Von, and I. Von wasn't here today, so Jeremy took his place.

September 14th, 1954 - Dear Diary, there isn't much time to be home any more. I hope I am learning something in that music class.

September 15th, 1954 - Dear Diary, we had a baseball game today. The Juniors and Seniors were beat. I was quite surprised. Jim and I and Christy went to the show.

September 16th, 1954 - Dear Diary, no more assigned seats in History, I was informed. They have taken Mark to Salt Lake for an operation.

My Dearest Diary

September 17th, 1954 - Dear Diary, in our music class we all had to lead "The Wintery Night" for our test. I was quite scared.

September 18th, 1954 - Dear Diary, we graduated class tonight. I hope I have learned something useful and can remember it.

September 19th, 1954 - Dear Diary, today I taught Wendy's class in Sunday school. My, I had a hard time!

September 20th, 1954 - Dear Diary, I don't know why some people do the things they do. Two boys left class yesterday in Sunday school.

September 21st, 1954 - Dear Diary, Rita and I went to Kanab to see the dentist today. We missed two classes. I got some shopping done.

September 22nd, 1954 - Dear Diary, the baseball team went to Enterprise for a ballgame. Almost all of the boys would rather play football, but we can't.

September 23rd, 1954 - Dear Diary, we lost the game by about 20 points! Darn our luck. Lane broke his finger, etc.

September 24th, 1954 - Dear Diary, we had an F.F.A. and F.H.A. party at Zion. It was a nice party, with the exception that the F.F.A. president didn't do as I would have liked to see him do.

September 25th, 1954 - Dear Diary, last night I thought I would croak! My how Jeremy acted!! Darn him. Oh, and we had an assembly. I sang "Three Coins in a Fountain."

September 26th, 1954 - Dear Diary, I went to Sunday school and meeting and fireside. Jim Berry talked. No, Jeremy didn't go to Sunday school. Wonder why?

September 27th, 1954 - Dear Diary, we had a ballgame today with Tropic. We were beat 11 to 4.

September 28th, 1954 - Dear Diary, we had a game with Escalante. It was a very good game, but Duane hurt his arm, and we were beat by three points.

September 29th, 1954 - Dear Diary, Algebra is going to be my biggest worry of all my classes, I believe, if I take Chorus part time or a lesson.

September 30th, 1954 - Dear Diary, we had a party for Seminary tonight. Guess what? Jeremy and Jenny are going to the dance tomorrow. How do I feel?

October 1st, 1954 - Dear Diary, it wasn't so bad after all. It is just one of those things, but then darn it!

October 2nd, 1954 - Dear Diary, as usual we cleaned house and washed in the rain. We went to the show "President's Lady."

October 3rd, 1954 - Dear Diary, we went to a party for Grandma at Cedar Canyon after Sunday School. We went to Cedar Breaks too.

October 4th, 1954 - Dear Diary, it is Lincoln's (19) birthday today. He does not get to go to college after all. He is pretty blue, and I don't blame him.

October 5th, 1954 - Dear Diary, in M.I.A. we had a very good lesson. It seemed nice to have a teacher again. I hope Ramona C. will be ours.

October 6th, 1954 - Dear Diary, we are out of school for a while, for U.E.A. It will seem good for a change. We went only ½ day today.

October 7th, 1954 - Dear Diary, it has been raining today, but we have still been busy with apples, pears, and tomatoes. My, we have a lot!

A Fancy

I have a fancy.
Just a dream of the heart.
In my fancy, there is someone to act the part.

I fancy a lover.
In fancy's dream, he lives.
Oh, sweet fancy,
To me, love happily he gives.

Wonderful fancy!
He loves no other but me.
In this dream,
No faults or imperfection I see.

Nor in true fancy,
Can anyone be found sad.
In my dream,
Completeness and joy will be had.

October 8th, 1954 - Dear Diary, what a day! It suddenly began to storm about noon. We did not have much damage, but oh what a flood at Orderville!

October 9th, 1954 - Dear Diary, it really piled up junk and destroyed downtown! I went down to see if I could get someone to help me with a song for tomorrow.

October 10th, 1954 - Dear Diary, I have been trying to get the mumps (I guess) all day. Well, I don't get to sing after all, but darn it, maybe I will really be sick.

October 11th, 1954 - Dear Diary, I stayed home today, but I really don't know why. I am not so sick. It seemed good anyway, for a change.

October 12th, 1954 - Dear Diary, I was set apart for a song leader of M.I.A. tonight. Isn't that wonderful! I hope I do not disappoint anyone and will learn to do it well.

October 13th, 1954 - Dear Diary, we are having troubles again! Those darn ornery boys will not cooperate! We can't decide on a theme for our dance.

October 14th, 1954 - Dear Diary, the Junior boys are learning how to date! But Jeremy's mother does not approve of Jenny.

October 15th, 1954 - Dear Diary, I went to the dance. Just another darn dance.

October 16th, 1954 - Dear Diary, we worked all day (as usual), then we went to the show "Titanic." Oh, it was sad. Everybody cried.

October 17th, 1954 - Dear Diary, it has been a good Sunday today. We all went to church. Almost everyone is very disappointed about Mr. D. He has been living lies.

October 18th, 1954 - Dear Diary, I went to a leadership in Kanab tonight. It was very nice. I think I am really going to like this!

October 19th, 1954 - Dear Diary, we certainly have good M.I.A. classes now. Romona C. is our teacher. I went to a prayer meeting and a leader's meeting.

October 20th, 1954 - Dear Diary, after all the Juniors' disagreement, I hope we have come to one conclusion. Our dance theme is finally decided, "The Happy Wanderer."

October 21st, 1954 - Dear Diary, tonight was the Deer Hunters' Ball. I didn't go. I was just too discouraged, and I didn't have anything to wear.

October 22nd, 1954 - Dear Diary, we had the Freshmen initiation into F.H.A. and the sleeping party. It was quite fun.

October 23rd, 1954 -Dear Diary, besides the other work, I picked up walnuts. We really have a lot. We kids went to "Shane."

October 24th, 1954 -Dear Diary, I went to Sunday school and meeting then to fireside at Christie's for M.I.A. leadership.

October 25th, 1954 - Dear Diary, my jaw hurts a little, but I had to go to school anyway. Tonight the Errings came to see us.

October 26th, 1954 - Dear Diary, I guess I have the mumps, but only on one side. I should have told a story in M.I.A. tonight.

October 27th, 1954 - Dear Diary, a number of the students have mumps. Yes, Jeremy has them. I'm sorry. He hated so much to get them. I hope he will not be very sick.

October 28th, 1954 - Dear Diary, now that I am home for a while, I get quite a bit of my reading etc. done. In a way, it seems good. Mike had a party.

October 19th, 1954 - Dear Diary, it seems sort of lonesome today. I sure enjoy Rita's letters. I drew a picture today, and I have read about a half dozen different things.

October 30th, 1954 - Dear Diary, it is good to have Wendy home on Saturdays, in more ways than one.

October 31st, 1954 - Dear Diary, I didn't go anyplace again today. I can usually find enough to do, but today I did get a little restless.

November 1st, 1954 - Dear Diary, I have ironed all day today. It seems good to be able to accomplish something. I must be getting better.

November 2nd, 1954 - Dear Diary, well back to school again. I know I will have to catch up on some studies.

November 3rd, 1954 - Dear Diary, we sure had a fun time tonight in an F.H.A. party! It takes exactly one week to get over one sided mumps.

November 4th, 1954 - Dear Diary, we are about to start to get ready for our dance. If we could only get along together!

November 5th, 1954 - Dear Diary, it was our dance tonight. As we expected, we had trouble from ornery, stubborn ones who would not do anything to help (or come to the dance).

November 6th, 1954 - Dear Diary, well, we didn't have a large crowd last night. All the Juniors weren't there either. Some are very uncooperative. I stayed at Rita's.

November 7th, 1954 - Dear Diary, what a wonderful conference! I hope I can remember it. Milton R. Hunter was there. I need to make a few resolutions, I know.

November 8th, 1954 - Dear Diary, guess what?! Our sweaters are here. I think they are very pretty. They are grey with black and orange.

November 9th, 1954 - Dear Diary, what a commotion we caused! Everyone seems to dislike grey. The boys have black sweaters, so everybody takes sides in our quarrels!

November 10th, 1954 - Dear Diary, some of our Junior boys really have me worried! I can't help but wonder about these dates with Jenny and Dolly. Are they good for Jeremy? Just what is he learning from them?

November 12th, 1954 - Dear Diary, today in school we had an assembly and a matinee dance. It was "The Dance," kind of stupid.

November 13th, 1954 - Dear Diary, even if all I get done on Saturdays is work that is soon undone, I enjoy it.

November 14th, 1954 - Dear Diary, we are really having the rounds. Wendy has been quite sick for some time, and Ikie and Sammy really have the mumps.

November 15th, 1954 - Dear Diary, school studies are about to "get me down." I'm so behind, yet so busy. I went to leadership.

November 16th, 1954 - Dear Diary, tonight in M.I.A. we planned a party for New Year's. It doesn't seem that near to Christmas already.

November 17th, 1954 - Dear Diary, it is different this year. Teachers don't seem the same (some of them are different). Mr. Jameson is sometimes hard to understand. I never have the time I need to get things done.

November 18th, 1954 - Dear Diary, in school today we saw the show "Rawhide." It wasn't so very good. It was too western and wild.

November 19th, 1954 - Dear Diary, tonight was the Orderville, Alton, Glendale, and Mt. Carmel Gold and Green Ball. I sang in a trio "Shine on Harvest Moon."

November 20th, 1954 - Dear Diary, Wendy and I went to a 4-H banquet at Roy's and Allison's café. It really was nice! (It is something to profit by).

November 21st, 1954 - Dear Diary, Jeremy is a priest now. Goodness, it seems like the boys are growing up fast! Jeremy and Dolly go with each other quite often.

November 22nd, 1954 - Dear Diary, Ikie and Sammy are over the mumps, so now two more have them (Roger and Mike).

November 23rd, 1954 - Dear Diary, I didn't get to go to M.I.A. tonight. Wendy had to go to Kanab to see the doctor and didn't get back.

November 24th, 1954 - Dear Diary, in school we had another matinee dance. It is fun to dance with girls. I am looking forward to a few days away from school.

November 25th, 1954 - Dear Diary, it has been a nice Thanksgiving, considering Lincoln and Daddy's coming down with the mumps, and my throat is sore.

November 26th, 1954 - Dear Diary, we had a party at the Easton's. It really was a lot of fun!

November 27th, 1954 - Dear Diary, Daddy and Lincoln are pretty sick. They really have the mumps! Mike, Roger, Mary Ann, and, I believe, Sammy all have it too.

November 28th, 1954 - Dear Diary, Wendy, Ikie, and I are the only ones who went anyplace today. Our house is full of mumps.

November 29th, 1954 - Dear Diary, it certainly is getting cold now. I guess it is time for winter.

November 30th, 1954 - Dear Diary, we went to a Mothers and Daughters meeting in Kanab. It really was good. Everyone feels bad tonight. Eva Hardy suddenly died.

December 1st, 1954 - Dear Diary, the Hardy family will have to be broken up. Evelyn is the only one to finish school in Orderville.

December 2nd, 1954 - Dear Diary, it doesn't seem like December yet!

December 3rd, 1954 - Dear Diary, there is nothing tonight for a change, but studies to do, and of course I need them. Algebra is my hardest class. I got the lowest mark I have ever had in it. I feel awful about it. I should know better than to get a C+ (in anything).

December 5th, 1954 - Dear Diary, I stayed down to Rita's tonight, until fireside. It was a wonderful fireside we had too. Guy and Reva Cornellia are just home from a mission.

December 6th, 1954 - Dear Diary, I am rather, or we are rather, worried about Wednesday night's performance. "Indian Love Call" is very pretty, but the verse is also very hard to learn.

December 7th, 1954 - Dear Diary, we saw two one-act plays tonight in M.I.A., and our ward had a conference. It all made a pretty good Mutual. Daddy is sick again; he got up too soon and his mumps fell.

December 8th, 1954 - Dear Diary, tonight was the band and chorus concert. Lane and I dressed as Indians and sang "Indian Love Call." It is something I have always wanted to do!

December 9th, 1954 - Dear Diary, I wasn't very scared last night when we sang, and I don't think Lane was. It was really quite a success, and many said they enjoyed it.

December 10th, 1954 - Dear Diary, we had our first home ballgame. We didn't win, but it still was a very good game. Dale did wonderful (16 points)! I danced with Mark for the first time (since he was hurt) tonight. He did not dance with Wendy, though I think he had a chance.

December 11th, 1954 - Dear Diary, with the house remodeling we had quite a hectic Saturday cleaning. Oh, but it will seem nice to have a nicer house! Mark came with Clarence Spencer tonight, when he came to get his milk. Wendy was upstairs writing to L., so I went to the door.

December 12th, 1954 - Dear Diary, Michael was sleigh riding today, and he ran into the pickup. He really bumped his head. He has a very bad gash.

December 13th, 1954 - Dear Diary, every Monday, Wednesday, and Friday some of us go early to school to practice for a Seminary program (23rd).

December 14th, 1954 - Dear Diary, tonight I feel so – Oh! I can't explain it. So different, about like I did a long time ago in the 8th grade. It is hard to explain. "Wonderful, maybe." But this sounds too young-ish and silly, but really it is so. I went to a play in Glendale.

December 15th, 1954 - Dear Diary, tonight was the game with Piute. Darn it! We were beaten again. So far we haven't won any basketball games.

December 16th, 1954 - Dear Diary, I stayed down after my lesson at Luanne's. We had a good time singing and making candy. Finally, the folks (mine) came, and I went shopping.

December 17th, 1954 - Dear Diary, at the dance tonight I really had a good time! Mark didn't come until quite late, but when he did, he danced with me twice. I danced with Jink, Lincoln, Ikie, and Paul too.

December 18th, 1954 - Dear Diary, I was really tired by the end of the dance. Tonight I am about as tired. I guess I need to catch up on sleep.

December 19th, 1954 - Dear Diary, I certainly feel good today. Really, I'm happy! A wonderful feeling.

December 20th, 1954 - Dear Diary, Elizabeth, Mark's cousin, wants to help me. She gives quite some information! She thinks she can replace a picture for me.

December 21st, 1954 - Dear Diary, what fun we had tonight at our M.I.A. party. Everyone had a good time with the games and "White Elephants."

December 22nd, 1954 - Dear Diary, these days sure seem to be busy ones. I can hardly find time enough to do all I need to, and Christmas is so near.

December 23rd, 1954 - Dear Diary, oh! I went to another dance tonight after the program. I really had fun again! I was afraid Mark wasn't going to come, but he finally did! Afterward, there was a party at Donna's (it is now 2:00).

December 24th, 1954 - Dear Diary, it seems like it is not quite time for Christmas already. Tonight we did the Christmas shopping, went to a program, and stayed up late getting ready for tomorrow.

December 25th, 1954 - Dear Diary, we had a wonderful Christmas! So much better than we had even hoped for. What surprises. Daddy really played Santa! Tonight there was a good dance.

December 26th, 1954 - Dear Diary, tonight I sang "The Holy City" in Glendale sacrament meeting. Everyone seemed to like it. Guess who told me hello? – the one who I danced twice with last night.

December 27th, 1954 - Dear Diary, tonight was another night out. We had a family party at Heaton's, just the kids. It was quite fun.

December 28th, 1954 - Dear Diary, guess what! I went to the show "Knock on Wood" and the Gold and Green Ball in Kanab with Mark. I really had a good time!

December 29th, 1954 - Dear Diary, tonight I am going to bed, for a change, at about 10:00. I did not get up this morning. It was about noon. Neither did Wendy. She had a date too.

December 30th, 1954 - Dear Diary, we have been quilting about all day today on Wendy's project. Aunt Eva has been helping us.

December 31st, 1954 - Dear Diary, I stayed home tonight. I guess I have had "my share" of fun for a while. Wendy and Lincoln went to a party and dance. I was not invited. I had a good time with the family making candy.

Memorandum

Dear Diary, 1954 has been quite a wonderful year! I have had a few heartaches and "blues," but lately it has all been worth it. I won't be 16 much longer. It seems like the time has gone so fast! Last year I hoped 1954 would bring what was needed. It has brought and fulfilled many things.

1955

January 1st, 1955

Dear Diary, tonight I went to the show "White Witch Doctor" and to the dance with Mark. What a good way of starting out the New Year! Don't you think so? Mark really is nice! Extraordinarily so.

January 2nd, 1955 - Dear Diary, it has really been snowing today. Lincoln went to Cedar to start school. We will sure miss him this winter.

Dear Diary, it seems to me these last few years have gone by so fast, and yet it is good to remember and realize what they have brought.

The snow is falling outside and all is white. I am thinking of the good and fun times I have had this season, some in snowy weather, and some in weather of spring.

I am starting this year out right – I am happy. It is much better to feel this way, than the way I remember starting out some years. I recall how I felt in 1952. Why that was actually 3 years ago! I must have been only in the 8th grade. Now I am a Junior in high school. Yes, I remember the cause of so many heartaches – my case on Nathan. Today, I realize they were also caused through growing up. Do I sound as if I knew all about it and am beyond stages of growing up? I know I am not. There are many things I have yet to learn. Probably there are more heartaches in store for me that I am to overcome. How many years does it take to grow up? That is a question unanswered. I think I will always be growing, not in just body, but I hope mind and ability as well.

Last night I had a date with Mark Pine. It was the second time I had gone with him. He is different from many boys. I am proud to be with him, and I know he will help me. I can trust him. He is sweet and un-spoiled. He is natural and nice to everyone. I hope I can help Mark. Since he was hurt, he cannot go to school or work for a year. I do not want to disappoint him or lose his respect. It makes one wonder why such things happen. Maybe it is to help him appreciate more.

Remember 1953, and I must add, a lot of 1954, when I wondered if and when I would ever get over the bumps in the road and have a chance at smooth going? I believe life must have its bumps and falls if we are to develop and grow. Maybe this year I will have more chances to appreciate. I hope so, but if it has many disappointments, I hope I can remember they are to help me, not hinder my progress. Oh, if I could only remember these things when I so need them.

This past year has added a lot to my life. This year of "sweet sixteen" with all of its hours of joy and sadness. It seems sixteen is a poetic year – so full of grandness! In a way this is like a poem, though I did not mean it to be. It is just emotions of mine.

January 3rd, 1955 - Dear Diary, back to school again and the old routine. It is good to see the kids again but hard to get settled down to work again after a few holidays.

January 4th, 1955 - Dear Diary, Lincoln took the car to Cedar, so we could not go to M.I.A. Everyone stayed home tonight, and we made cookies and popped corn.

January 5th, 1955 - Dear Diary, Mrs. Jameson came and got me to go to singing at Mothers and Daughters in Glendale tonight. It was quite a time.

January 6th, 1955 - Dear Diary, tonight I had a "prom" permanent. Last night, Elizabeth and Helen thought they had a sleigh riding party planned.

January 7th, 1955 - Dear Diary, I went to the ballgame and dance tonight. We were beaten again by about 20 points. Mark came to the dance later. I only danced with him once.

January 8th, 1955 - Dear Diary, I have been filling out a 4-H report in hopes of winning a scholarship. All day.

January 9th, 1955 - Dear Diary, it seemed good to have all of us together again for Sunday school. Then Lincoln left for college. I don't know when we will see him again.

January 10th, 1955 - Dear Diary, there really is quite a lot of snow now a days. We had a home evening tonight. Times like these make it all worthwhile.

January 11th, 1955 - Dear Diary, we are finally starting on the new gym! January 7th we had breaking ceremonies in the old gym because it was snowing.

January 12th, 1955 - Dear Diary, Mark has the mumps. Oh dear! I hope he takes care of himself and doesn't let them make him very sick.

January 13th, 1955 - Dear Diary, I had a lesson tonight, the first one in weeks. Wendy did not come and get me, so guess who brought me home? Paul H.

January 14th, 1955 - Dear Diary, Lane and I sang "Indian Love Call" tonight in a poultry meeting. It went quite well. I sent a get well card to Mark. Do you think that was stupid of me?

January 15th, 1955 - Dear Diary, Roy and Allison came to see us today. They want the piano back because Roy is studying music.

January 16th, 1955 - Dear Diary, it is snowing hard again. We went to Sunday school but just about did not get home! We didn't try going to meeting.

January 17th, 1955 - Dear Diary, in school today we saw "Mr. Belvedere goes to College." The building is really getting torn apart! Mrs. Hansen is about over the mumps.

January 18th, 1955 - Dear Diary, we are getting more snow again. We were lucky to be able to go to M.I.A. for the first time in 1955. We had a wonderful lesson on marriage.

January 19th, 1955 - Dear Diary, things surely seem hectic, not a bit natural. We have classes all over the campus and plenty of studies. At home we have arguments.

January 20th, 1955 - Dear Diary, what a day! I will have to tell it on more paper than what is here –

Dear Diary, what a day! First, Rita brought a big birthday present to school for me. That always makes me feel like I am getting more than I deserve. So many of the kids wished me a happy birthday.

Second, Mr. James caused trouble. He has assigned 10,000-word reference themes that are to be written in what we thought was a peculiar way. He did not understand it himself, it appeared, because he contradicted himself. After some of the girls had written them already once or twice, he then changed his mind. They were plenty discouraged. The next class we discussed it. Arlene began to cry. The tears rolled down Phyllis's cheeks. Then Rose and Gwenda cried, and then Rita and Madeline and Joy. Jenny and I joined them. We all had to go to the dressing room for a few minutes.

After class was out, we went to talk to him and "have it out." I did not feel as bad as some of them. A few of us looked at each other and wondered if we dare go in. He had explained it to me, and I understood part of his method. We did not wait long. Arlene (she is one of the shyest, but she was the maddest) led the way. She began to really tell him what she thought. Arlene was crying all the while. Gwenda joined in, the tears streaming down her cheeks and dripping on her (darn) English reference books. Joy and Rita were talking as loud as the other two. The rest of us just stood.

Somehow I felt sorry for Mr. James. He tried to answer as best he could. I had secretly hoped he would cry too, but he did not. However, he was a bit confused, and I don't blame him. I believe I have said before that he is very "different!" That is what makes him hard to understand.

Third, I stayed down for a music lesson. Wendy did not come to get me for a long time. I was just going to Rita's when Wendy came to get me. We went to Roy's to get some pictures. We were there for about 1 ½ hours. We went home, and she said we could go to the M-men basketball game. Mama was making me a cake. I found a card and picture from Mark! Oh boy.

Fourth, well we went to the ballgame, that is, we started there. Wendy said we were to stop at Rita's and take her with us. When I ask her if she was going with us, I heard a shout. There was a surprise birthday party for me. Oh, it was nice! There was even a cake with 17 candles. The party lasted until quite late. The rest of the family came to the party. Everyone had cake and ice cream.

My seventeenth birthday was a day to remember.

January 21st, 1955 - Dear Diary, what a contrast! I feel about as ornery as possible. Kanab won the basketball game and ruined the stupid dance!!

January 22nd, 1955 - Dear diary, today Uncle Neldon and Jack and Jim built cupboard doors for us. Mama and Wendy went to a party. What a time!

January 23rd, 1955 - Dear Diary, we went to Sunday school and meeting. Dee took some things over to Lincoln at Cedar.

January 24th, 1955 - Dear Diary, Miss Crawford is sick now. School is mixed up again. We got our grades. I got A's except B in Home Ec. and C in Algebra.

January 25th, 1955 - Dear Diary, in M.I.A. we had a Silver Gleaner program. It really was something to remember. Times when we get together and learn and have fun are nice to have.

January 26th, 1955 - Dear Diary, Miss Crawford has the mumps or the flu. She won't be to school for a week or so. It seems funny without band or chorus.

January 27th, 1955 - Dear Diary, Lincoln phoned Wendy and has a blind date all arranged with Owen for her. I delivered calendars tonight.

January 28th, 1955 - Dear Diary, it has been quite a night. We almost beat Enterprise 45 – 50. A very exciting game and a pretty good dance. A much bigger improvement over last week's. Lincoln was here and Mark.

January 29th, 1955 - Dear Diary, I didn't do much today. We cleaned yesterday, so this Saturday I got some studying done and caught up on rest and being lazy.

January 30th, 1955 - Dear Diary, today we went to Sunday school and testimony meeting. We Jr. Gleanors sang "Whither Thou Goest."

January 31st, 1955 - Dear Diary, the school building is being constantly torn down or remodeled. Talk about noise and tobacco!

February 1st, 1955 - Dear Diary, it seems I am certainly not doing my duty in M.I.A. I have only lead the singing once and neither dare or had the chance again.

February 2nd, 1955 - Dear Diary, I must say this year is the hardest yet. I mean in the learning responsibilities, for instance Algebra. I almost hate it!

February 3rd, 1955 - Dear Diary, I stayed at Rita's tonight for flower making. We have the craziest boys in our class! Merrill, Duane, Al, and Marlynn were there.

February 4th, 1955 - Dear Diary, the chorus had an assembly today. I sang "The Lord's Prayer" for a devotional number. I practiced only once before.

February 5th, 1955 - Dear Diary, I went with Mark to an Elder's conference and social in Kanab. It was very nice, and we had a good time.

February 6th, 1955 - Dear Diary, we (Mama, Wendy and Ikie and me and Roger) went to afternoon session of conference. Then Roger and I came home. Mama and Ikie and Wendy stayed to a scout meeting.

February 7th, 1955 - Dear Diary, life and things are quite wonderful aren't they? If we but remember they are and don't let small worries bother us.

February 8th, 1955 - Dear Diary, for M.I.A. there was a Valentine party in the gym. Rita has the mumps. Paul said he had intended to take her to the Elder's social.

February 9th, 1955 - Dear Diary, I got the part of Mary in "Mississippi Melody," an operetta. Golly! I'm glad. I'll bet it will really be fun being in one.

February 10th, 1955 - Dear Diary, I have quite the premonitions! Three times I thought Mark would come, and every time he has come as I was thinking it. It is quite a way.

February 11th, 1955 - Dear Diary, we have had two tests today. Three were scheduled. We were out of school by 3:00. The bus left for Hurricane at 4:00.

February 12th, 1955 - Dear Diary, tonight I went to the show with Mark. Guess what he gave me afterwards! A box of candy and card for Valentine's. I am making him one.

February 13th, 1955 - Dear Diary, we went to Sunday school meeting and fireside today. Wendy and I made Valentines this morning to send to Mark and Lynn.

February 14th, 1955 - Dear Diary, in Home Ec. what a fun Valentine's Day party. I opened my candy tonight. Gosh! That was nice of Mark! I hope he has a happy Valentine's Day and likes the one I sent.

February 15th, 1955 - Dear Diary, Mutual certainly teaches a lot and helps our way of thinking. Afterwards, Mama and Daddy and Wendy and I talked and discussed.

February 16th, 1955 - Dear Diary, today we saw the show "Deseret Song." It was really a good show, even if we have to wait until tomorrow to see the last part.

February 17th, 1955 - Dear Diary, after my lesson I played at Luanne's until Wendy came for me. Mark had been up home to see me. He came again later.

February 18th, 1955 - Dear Diary, I went with Mark to the Kanab and Valley game and dance. Kanab won by a number of points, but that didn't ruin the night.

February 19th, 1955 - Dear Diary, I went to Alton to a dance with Mark and Dee and Rita and Laverne and Jim and Edith.

February 20th, 1955 - Dear Diary, I have been tired all day. Too much night life, I guess. It was so cold in Alton. I have a cold.

February 21st, 1955 - Dear Diary, I stayed home from a dance tonight. I didn't feel a bit like going, and I have two books to finish by Friday.

February 22nd, 1955 - Dear Diary, it didn't seem much like a holiday today. Too many studies and tending kids and lambs and work.

February 23rd, 1955 - Dear Diary, we all went to the show "Robin Hood" tonight. It really seemed good, and it was an enjoyable show.

February 24th, 1955 - Dear Diary, I've come to the conclusion: I could work at studies every hour I am home and still not get it done. This is the busiest year!

February 25th, 1955 - Dear Diary, in school we are having term tests. It is Algebra I dread most.

February 26th, 1955 - Dear Diary, I like weekends. Wonder why! I went with Mark to the Sweethearts Ball. Mama and Wendy went too.

February 27th, 1955 - Dear Diary, meeting was good tonight. Aunt Vera and Uncle Guy Cornellia talked about their mission and the gospel. Later they and Bishop Coventon talked in fireside. It makes me want to go on a mission even more.

February 28th, 1955 - Dear Diary, we have been trying to make decisions about an exchange assembly. Between it, operetta practice, the Solo-Ensemble, studies, and parties like we had tonight at Aunt Orvillia's, I feel almost in a worried dither!

February 29th, 1955 - Dear Diary, tonight for the second time, I lead the singing in M.I.A. It isn't so bad after all. I think I could learn to really enjoy it! We had a wonderful lesson on "Temple Marriage." Ramona told us of 3 different kinds of weddings.

March 1st, 1955 - Dear Diary, we had an operetta practice again tonight. I'll bet this is really going to be worth it!

March 2nd, 1955 - Dear Diary, I wonder if all Junior years are like mine is. Sometimes it is cram full of worries, sometimes cram full of wonderfulness!

March 3rd, 1955 - Dear Diary, Wendy and some other F.H.A. officers went to Salt Lake for a convention. I am to take Wendy's place as reporter.

March 4th, 1955 - Dear Diary, I went with Mark and his folks to the game and dance. Then we reported the game to Cedar.

March 5th, 1955 - Dear Diary, I have been tired all day. I heard we won a game with Kanab! I was too busy and tired to go, but don't get me wrong, sometimes I don't mind being tired.

My Dearest Diary

March 6th, 1955 - Dear Diary, I went to Sunday school and meeting. We had a family party for Mary Ann and fireside here tonight. I wish weeks had more than a weekend.

March 7th, 1955 - Dear Diary, we practiced the operetta after school. Later, Ora May and I went to Orderville and practiced our festival numbers. Mine is "Lullaby."

Dear Diary, I really do like Mark. Some of my feelings are hard to explain. Thoughts of him disturb me, yet being with him calms me. He is really a help that way. Is it the real him I like or is it something in my mind's eye? You know what I mean – Don't you? Something I made up or dreamed. I have done it before and found lots of made up dreams don't come true, but now I have more of a chance to know what I am dreaming about.

March 8th, 1955 - Dear Diary, guess who is working at the gym? We presented our assembly today. After school, I practiced some more. I said hello to Mark afterwards.

March 9th, 1955 - Dear Diary, I am tired tonight. It has been a full day. Eight or ten of us went to Hurricane for the Solo-Ensemble. Some of us felt we could have done our parts better.

March 10th, 1955 - Dear Diary, we have had quite a time today in our first Jr. Prom dance practice (and disagreements) also operetta practice.

March 11th, 1955 - Dear Diary, during school we planned a surprise party for Rita. After school, we practiced operetta. It has been raining today.

March 12th, 1955 - Dear Diary, I made Rita a cake, we went down to her place at 6:00, and five of us girls had a party. Later, two more came, then we went to "Come Back, Little Sheba."

March 13th, 1955 - Dear Diary, Mama, Wendy, Daddy, and Lincoln all went to Cedar. I stayed home. Tonight, Bill and Ikie went to Glendale meeting, so I did too. Then Wendy and I went to fireside tonight.

March 14th, 1955 - Dear Diary, Mark is still working at school on the new gym, so I get to see him working sometimes between classes.

March 15th, 1955 - Dear Diary, the boys came to our M.I.A. class. They caused such a disturbance, they had to leave. It is just too bad.

March 16th, 1955 - Dear Diary, we presented our operetta at noon for the grade school and junior high. It didn't go very well.

March 17th, 1955 - Dear Diary, tonight was the operetta. We will never forget it. It really was an experience! The first I have had of that kind. Remember how always I have looked forward to it?

March 18th, 1955 - Dear Diary, I went to "Lost in Alaska" at Glendale with Mark. Then we went to his place while he got ready for the dance (Senior Ball). A night to remember.

March 19th, 1955 - Dear Diary, Mark took me to a dance at Hatch. We went with Jessie and Merrill. Somehow it seemed different. I will try to get to tell you more about it (but not tonight).

March 20th, 1955 - Dear Diary, I dared to wear my high heels to church today. It was a bit hard walking. We went to fireside at Lane's. Grandma and Bob and Orvilla came. Grandma gave me $5 for a prom dress.

March 21st, 1955 - Dear Diary, there is a party for Jeremy tonight, but I am staying home to see if I can feel better for the exchange assembly tomorrow. I need more sleep.

March 22nd, 1955 - Dear Diary, we took our exchange assembly to Hurricane, then Cedar today. I was sorry I didn't get to see Lincoln, but we just didn't have time afterwards.

March 23rd, 1955 - Dear Diary, Kanab was very nice to us when we took the assembly there this morning. We were quite surprised.

March 24th, 1955 - Dear Diary, it will be hard to get back into a schedule again. With all of these extra things, it is not easy to study again. Mama and I went to "Oliver Cowdery" in Glendale.

March 25th, 1955 - Dear Diary, I sang "Make Believe" again, this time in a farewell dance at Mt. Carmel. No, Mark was not there, but his Aunt Libby was there.

March 26th, 1955 - Dear Diary, I still like weekends best of all. Mark and I went to "From Showboat to Broadway." His mother and Aunt (Maurine) went with us. Later we two went to "All the Brothers Were Valiant."

March 27th, 1955 - Dear Diary, there was a wonderful meeting tonight. It was a M.I.A. speech festival (about temples and God) like the one I saw in Salt Lake in June. I helped sing "Oh, my Father" as a quartet.

March 28th, 1955 - Dear Diary, have I told you of the opera in Cedar the 30th and 31st? I had resolved at the exchange assembly to get back to Cedar and shop for a formal and maybe see it. The Seminary is going Thursday.

March 29th, 1955 - Dear Diary, it has been stake election for the Jr. Gleaners and men in Kanab tonight. I was our candidate and so was Al. He won.

March 30th, 1955 - Dear Diary, guess what?! I am almost sure our scheme will work. Mama and Daddy have finally consented. Now – if only things work out.

March 31st, 1955 - Dear Diary, we really had a good time tonight. I went with Mr. C to Cedar to "The Silver Chalice." Then Phyllis and I stayed in Cedar.

April 1st, 1955 - Dear Diary, Phyllis and I went shopping until noon (I found a formal). Lincoln came to see me at Jean's at 12:00. We ate then went to his apartment. I met one of his roommates, Barten.

April 2nd, 1955 - Dear Diary, last night we came home about 6:00. I went to the dance. I didn't have any fun except talking with the girls and laughing at jokes. I stayed home tonight.

April 3rd, 1955 - Dear Diary, I went to Sunday school and meeting. There was a meeting afterward to decide on an M.I.A. dance. I am chairman.

April 4th, 1955 - Dear Diary, the Seniors had their sluff today. Some of us Juniors went to Kanab for a Home Ec. class. We went to the cleaners.

April 5th, 1955 - Dear Diary, we were supposed to dance in M.I.A. (if we had partners). Rita and I made Jr. Prom signs. I have to use every bit of my time.

April 6th, 1955 - Dear Diary, there are so many things to be done! I can't help but wonder if everything will come out right.

April 7th, 1955 - Dear Diary, I went to Cedar tonight and saw the opera "The New Moon." It was very good, the first in Cedar's new building.

April 8th, 1955 - Dear Diary, I took Mark to the Girls' Day dance. Lincoln came home. He went down with us. It seems so good to have him home. We had sort of a party after the dance.

April 9th, 1955 - Dear Diary, our kitchen was really changed today! We have been moving around stoves and tables and a refrigerator.

April 10th, 1955 - Dear Diary, we had a good Easter Sunday. Lincoln is home for the day. We had a picnic in Lydie's Canyon by the upper pond. Chick and Jean came.

April 11th, 1955 - Dear Diary, the lunch room is open again. It really seems good. I think everyone is tired of bringing their lunch.

April 12th, 1955 - Dear Diary, things are happening too fast! There is too much to do. Next I have to send out the Prom signs (make them first).

April 13th, 1955 - Dear Diary, the Juniors (that is some of us) are trying to learn the dance for the floor show before Prom night. It is quite a job.

April 14th, 1955 - Dear Diary, I am to be the honor student in Seminary graduation. That also calls for work (and worry).

April 15th, 1955 - Dear Diary, we were to have V day today, but it seems someone left their cleaning material home, so everyone went to school in jeans. Talk about mad! We had Junior assembly.

April 16th, 1955 - Dear Diary, some of us went to Cedar today for Vocational day. It was quite a trip to remember. I got my formal. Later tonight, I got my Junior Prom date too.

April 17th, 1955 - Dear Diary, we went to church today. Tonight Mama, Wendy, and I went to meeting. Wendy and I stayed to fireside.

April 18th, 1955 - Dear Diary, everybody is mad! Mr. Hansen is on the prod and so are Miss Crawford and Mr. Henderson. Tonight, we Juniors left it all and went to Kanab to "White Christmas."

April 19th, 1955 - Dear Diary, we really feel picked on and misstreated. The teachers bark at us, say we cause all the trouble, and won't let us have time to decorate.

April 20th, 1955 - Dear Diary, they finally let us in the gym. We got busy and really worked. I did not get home until after 11:00, tired and hungry.

April 21st, 1955 - Dear Diary, we are still wondering if we can get ready by tomorrow. I hope Mr. Hanson is worried!

April 22nd, 1955 - Dear Diary, after quite a day, we had our Prom. I can say all the fight, worry, suspense, and work was worth it. I don't believe it could have been better (for me).

Dear Diary, I cannot resist writing a note. This has been a wonderful night, although the day did not go so well.

At first, the teachers seemed to be against us. Mr. Hanson would not let us have a week to decorate. Miss Crawford did not want us to use the gym so early, Mr. Hanson said. She felt all Junior band students might cause the band to be ruined if they did not attend band regularly. Mr. Henderson felt the Junior boys were causing the ball team to be ruined. The boys are mad because of coach's actions and refuse to play.

Later on, I realized the teachers' attitudes brought the Juniors closer together. Believe me, we needed it.

The last few days were spent rushing to get things in order. The orchestra almost left us. That gave us a scare. We almost postponed the dance. We thought we didn't have enough paper. The teachers would not let us have a homeroom. In other words, there was considerable war.

My Dearest Diary

But the dance was worth it. Finally, the decorating was done and just in time too.

Everyone looked so nice. Mark had a new dark blue suit, and I had my formal. I wish you could see the corsage he gave me. This time, they were real roses. There are seven yellow buds tied with pink, lavender, and blue ribbons. They smell pretty too. The first part of the dance passed quickly, then it was time for the floorshow. I was quite scared, but everyone said I did well in both the dance and the theme song, "Beautiful Lady." It is thrilling to have some say they liked it and to feel it was a success. The dance went by so fast, I didn't realize it was over. Afterward there was a Junior party at Miss Easton's. We went until 1:30 and then came home.

I will always remember my Junior Prom, and it was worth it.

April 23rd, 1955 - Dear Diary, I was glad to go to bed earlier tonight. The week had been tiring. Even though it was, I am sorry it is over.

April 24th, 1955 - Dear Diary, we had a Silver Gleaner program tonight and a party at our teacher's home. Ramona Cornellia has certainly helped us.

April 25th, 1955 - Dear Diary, if I am to get my projects for Seminary completed, I must get on the ball.

April 26th, 1955 - Dear Diary, our lessons in M.I.A. are really wonderful! We are taught that if we go wrong, it will be our own fault, not our teachers' or parents'.

April 27th, 1955 - Dear Diary, tonight I finally finished my Seminary project on The Presidents of the Church. It has been enough work!

April 28th, 1955 - Dear Diary, tomorrow is going to be V day (believe me?). Seminary is getting to be a problem.

April 29th, 1955 - Dear Diary, Mark and I went to the post prom. Aren't I just so lucky!! To have him for a date, I mean. He does mean a lot (is it just growing up?).

April 30th, 1955 - Dear Diary, I got up tired this early morning. I hope Mark is not as tired as I am. I tended Aunt Eva's kids. I haven't been so darned tired for a long time.

May 1st, 1955 - Dear Diary, it seems so good to have Lincoln home for a whole. This afternoon Lincoln, Wendy, and I had a very good time talking and discussing together.

Dear Diary, it is the first of May already! I find it hard to believe. This weekend is also something to remember!

I was a little afraid I would not have a date for the Post Prom. I felt too, maybe I was wanting more of his dates than I deserved. He did ask me Friday night after work (The day had been a fun V day).

Mark came for me about 9:00. I was surprised to find we were going in Bob's car with him, Eva, and Nathan (did you say that name looks familiar?).

The dance was a lot like the Prom. To make it nicer, Lincoln was home so he was able to go to the dance

I danced with Mark, Lincoln, Bob, Sammy, Donald, and Mike.

We Junior girls had planned a girls sleeping party to be at Phylliss's after the dance. We were to bring our dates to the party before. I knew our being with Bob would cause complication, but Phyllis said it would be okay to invite them too. I almost did, then I found out Bob was taking Rahnell home after the dance. For some reason I felt very reluctant to invite Bob to come. Was it fair to have her to this party too? The more I thought about it, the more I disliked the idea. I soon realized however, I must invite Mark. It would be ignorant not to, and I wanted to invite him.

I told myself it might not really be so bad. She would have her date, and I would have mine. First, I asked Mark. Well, he solved the problem. He said he would have Bob take us home, and we would take his car. I wonder if Mark knew how relieved I was. After seeing the way Rahnell acts when she has a boy with her, I did not know why I should ever worry about Mark liking her very well. He doesn't seem to be the kind of a boy who would like that kind of girl. Nathan had a date also, with Vivian. She is young and sweet. Nathan was quite nice. It seemed good to see him again.

We found Mark's car and keys, came up home, got my things, and went to the party. Phyllis, Rose, Rita, and Caroline were the only ones there. They had on their jeans. I was the only one in a formal, and Mark was the only boy. I was afraid he might be embarrassed. He didn't seem to be at all. He talked with us, and it made the time pass sooner. Deanna, in her formal, and Duane came. We ate sandwiches, salad, pickles, potato chips, and cake (mine) and drank punch while we listened to records.

We waited a long time for Madeline and Lane to come. When their car drove up, we turned out the lights and the girls watched out the window. We watched and waited. Time went by. Mark said he had better go home. He had to work in the morning. Soon he and Duane left. We girls continued to wait for Madeline. The porch light was on. All others were turned off. We watched in the dark.

Finally, they came upon the porch. We had a hard time controlling our laughs. They stood there talking for some time. It wasn't much fun for us because we couldn't hear them. She came in after a while, and we made our beds. Two girls slept in two rooms and three slept in one room. The party had left few hours for sleep. We talked for a while, of course. By morning we were completely tired. What a way to wake up! And I had had such dreams!

I started walking home, and Bishop's wife brought me home. What a time!

Mark is, how can I say it, well, just real nice, and I really like him. He is extra so! I hope I always think he is wonderful. I hope he will always continue to like me, as he does now. Goodness! I hope I don't disappoint him. Oh, may I always seem sweet to him! I must remember Lincoln's advice.

May 2nd, 1955 - Dear Diary, the time is so rushed and full! It is hard to realize it passes so quickly. Maybe it is because I am so busy.

May 3rd, 1955 - Dear Diary, I was late for M.I.A. again. Last time I was too late to lead the singing. We will have to hurry more. It was a scout meeting. Bishop Pine talked.

May 4th, 1955 - Dear Diary, did I ever tell you it came to $45 in debt on the Proms. It is too bad, but it could be worse, I guess. Later: no we cleared about that much.

May 5th, 1955 - Dear Diary, in school we have been having a few ball games. They are not a bit good – we are beaten by dozens of points every time.

May 6th, 1955 - Dear Diary, we had an M.I.A. program and dance in Orderville. All of the family went together. The dance was not very crowded.

May 7th, 1955 - Dear Diary, it was the Spring Festival in Parowan today. And what a day it was. The chorus sang two songs.

May 8th, 1955 - Dear Diary, we have had quite a Mother's day! After church, we kids cooked dinner for Mama. I made a very feeble cake. Daddy bought ice cream.

May 9th, 1995 - Dear Diary, last night Wendy and I went to fireside with Donald and Guard, to settle up unfinished business, they said.

May 10th, 1955 - Dear Diary, school is really rushed! I am afraid my grades will fall short. I haven't time enough to do everything I should.

May 11th, 1955 - Dear Diary, I hardly ever ride home on the bus anymore, but I did tonight.

May 12th, 1955 - Dear Diary, I am helping make our Seminary decorations and program and preparing my talk on "Obedience and Forgiveness."

May 13th. 1955 - Dear Diary, tonight we graduated from Seminary. It was something I will never forget. I received a diploma and a "Book of Mormon."

May 14th, 1955 - Dear Diary, in spite of everything to think about, I miss Mark's dates. I see him at school. It seems to be worse. I wonder if I did something wrong? Will I get over how I feel?

May 15th, 1955 - Dear Diary, Wendy and I went to fireside again, with Guard and Donald. Guess where Guard asked me to go with Donald?

May 16th, 1955 - Dear Diary, Wendy and I had dates tonight with Guard and Donald. We went to the stake dance festival, then to the show.

May 17th, 1955 - Dear Diary, we didn't get home tonight from our dates until about 12:00. I should have studied.

May 18th, 1955 - Dear Diary, what a day for tests! History and Algebra didn't get studied last night. I am afraid I flunked my Algebra test. We all went to the grade school program.

May 19th, 1955 - Dear Diary, tonight was Wendy's graduation. The whole night was sad. I cried during graduation. I think quite a few did. No, I did not have a date. He wasn't even at the dance.

Dear Diary, today and tonight have been some of the bluest I have had to go through. It is difficult to say when it all began. I believe it has been accumulating for a while. I haven't gone with Mark since April 29th. I wonder what I did or did not do! I have gone with Donald (I haven't especially wanted to either), but what am I to do when he asks me, and he is nice?

Of course, Mark does know about it. Will it make any difference? The night I went with him I should have been home studying for an Algebra test. I found out today I flunked the test. That, and Miss Easton's attitude, was about all I could take. She was ornery about dressing in P.E. and wouldn't accept what I made in Home Ec. During Algebra I was so mad and befuddled I almost cried.

Elizabeth talked to me, and it helped some. She said Mark felt too tired to go with me after work and has to get up early (at 6:00) to work the next day. He didn't seem to let Donald's dates bother him, just made an eggy comment and said he would have to get on the ball. I wonder if he will. I thought he might take me to graduation.

All of the family (except Lincoln) went earlier and went together. He was there with his folks. I realize how selfish I had been in wishing he would have taken me. I was glad he went with them. We were late. Michael, Mary Ann, and I sat in the east wing. We could not see much. It was dark, I had a handkerchief, graduation was wonderful, and I needed it, so I really let the tears flow.

I had thought he would surely be to the dance; this last dance of the year, this last dance in the park. I was disappointed he did not ever come. But guess who was there? Yes, Donald was there. He and Miss Easton came together. Somehow I wanted to scream. I felt mad at them both. Most of the girls were there, and we talked. I kept reminiscing about Proms and thinking this is the very last of a wonderful year. Rita and Luanne thought I was too sentimental. Maybe I was. I still felt like crying and a few times almost did. I danced with Donald and Gerald. Some asked, "Where is Mark?" I said, "He must be home. I don't know." I hated to ride home on the bus, practically alone. Arlene, Gwenda, and Jenny all had ways home. Oh how I am learning to appreciate Mark. Am I appreciating too late?

May 20th, 1955 - Dear Diary, we all went to school this morning and got our things and came home at noon.

May 21st, 1955 - Dear Diary, Wendy, Luanne, and I went to the dance festival in St. George. Luanne and I had fun buying Wendy a present and looking at flowers and houses.

May 22nd, 1955 - Dear Diary, after meeting tonight, Guard said Donald wanted to see me. He asked me to go with him to a show Wednesday night. I shall.

May 23rd, 1955 - Dear Diary, we have been cleaning up both the yards and our room. Right in the middle of it, we left for Main Canyon where we had an F.H.A. party.

May 24th, 1955 - Dear Diary, today I again attempted to successfully raise a flower garden in the dog's favorite resting place, between the two paths. I led the singing in M.I.A.

May 25th, 1955 - Dear Diary, we went to Kanab to the show "The Bamboo Prison" about communism. It was not such a bad date. He gave me a lesson in driving.

May 26th, 1955 - Dear Diary, we had our first 4-H meeting yesterday. Lincoln and Dee will be coming home. Wendy and I hope to give them a party in Lydie's Canyon at the pond.

May 27th, 1955 - Dear Diary, we had the party. The boys fully enjoyed themselves. Mark had fun with his boy friends. It must have seemed good to him to have them back. I was glad to see them have fun.

May 28th, 1955 - Dear Diary, don't trust any premonition. They don't always prove true. I climbed the hill today and drew a view. I did not go to a show.

May 29th, 1955 - Dear Diary, it is good to have Lincoln home for a while. We three went to fireside and afterward had one of our talks. We discuss about everything.

May 30th, 1955 - Dear Diary, I know he had a day off today. I hope he really enjoyed it and caught a lot of fish. I write with no sarcasm. What right have I?

May 31st, 1955 - Dear Diary, Karen, Ora May, and Sherman are here for a while. Aunt Eva is having an operation. Wendy, Sammy, and I went to M.I.A.

Dear Diary, it has been a month and more since I have gone with Mark. I must have let him stay out too, too late April 29th, but he could have gone from the party anytime (not just at 3:00 in the morning). Do his folks think I am just a bit too much of a hussy? Or is it Mark does not care anymore?

June 1st, 1955 - Dear Diary, it snowed a little today! Karen, Ora May, Sherman, Mary Ann, and I went on the hill for a picnic of Karen's 4-H sandwiches. We have been reading.

June 2nd, 1955 - Dear Diary, I am cooking things for 4-H. We did some watering today. I furrowed rows for the peas and onions. Lincoln and Dee are planning dates for tomorrow.

June 3rd, 1955 - Dear Diary, tonight it turned out this way: Oral and Wendy, Dee and Rita, and Lincoln and me. Donald wanted me to drive him home. I didn't. I had a date. Mark was not there.

June 4th, 1955 - Dear Diary, Lorraine and Jay are here. Mama went to Cedar to see Eva. Wendy and I both made deals with a salesman. I hope we can carry them through.

June 5th, 1955 - Dear Diary, I went to Glendale to Sunday school with Karen and Ora May. He wasn't there! I don't know what to think.

June 6th, 1955 - Dear Diary, Wendy and I went to "The Robe" in Kanab with Guard and Donald. Donald is teaching me how to drive. He is a good teacher.

June 7th, 1955 - Dear Diary, Mama, Daddy, Guard, Donald, and I all went to the M.I.A. executive party. Wendy is at Aunt Eva's.

June 8th, 1955 - Dear Diary, I am going to stay and help Aunt Eva at her place in Glendale for a while. I shall prepare meals and help the kids.

June 9th, 1955 - Dear Diary, I got a letter from Arlene today. It seemed so good to hear from her. I have been asked to sing in a High Priest party.

June 10th, 1955 - Dear Diary, I have felt so blue all day. I wrote Arlene a sad letter. I miss everybody. I hardly ever see anyone. You know what I mean?

June 11th, 1955 - Dear Diary, I went with Mark to an Elder's party in the canyon. It was a very fun party! Jim, Amy, Dee, and Rita went with us. (I am not blue anymore). I am at Eva's.

Dear Diary, I haven't been so happy for weeks! I was with Mark again. Oh, it had seemed a long time since I had even seen him. Tonight I almost didn't get to go with him. I had been asked to sing in a High Priests party. When he asked me to go with him to the Elder's party, he said he thought the other party had been called off. I was glad. Jim, Amy, Dee, and Rita went with us. It was about the funnest party I have been to (or was I just happy?). It was late before we all finally got home.

June 12th, 1955 - Dear Diary, I went to church with Neldon and Eva and the kids. Liz arranged everything so Mark would sit by me in meeting. Glendale's meeting was good so was their Sunday school.

Dear Diary, I have always wanted to see Mark in Sunday school, when he sits in the front of the congregation. I have thought I could know more about him that way. This morning he was there. He looked as wonderful, clean, and good as I thought he would. He was almost radiant, I thought. Can it be he was feeling like I was. I was as happy as I could want to be. I often wonder if my feelings are extreme or are they natural?

June 13th, 1955 - Dear Diary, guess what! I have been stood up. I thought I had a date with Donald. Well, I don't care. I do need some sleep if I go to Las Vegas tomorrow.

June 14th, 1955 - Dear Diary, a group of us left to go to a dance festival in Las Vegas. It was an interesting trip down. We practiced and found a place to stay. Then we went to the festival.

June 15th, 1955 - Dear Diary, today has really been one to remember. We went with Watsons to Boulder Dam and Lake Mead then began the long drive home. We got here in the evening.

June 16th, 1955 - Dear Diary, this morning I went to Cedar with Mr. Rose and four others. We are to stay two nights in the ladies' dormitory for our older boys and girls 4-H club camp.

June 17th, 1955 - Dear Diary, we have had a busy day today. We had group singing, demonstrations, discussions, a party in the canyon, a campfire program, then dancing in the gym. (I am to be the secretary).

June 18th, 1955 - Dear Diary, we left Cedar today at about noon. Soon after I got home, Mark asked me to go to "Prince of Players" in Kanab.

Dear Diary, I went to the show tonight with Mark. His father and two of his sisters went with us. I am glad they went with us. I enjoyed talking with them.

Sometimes Mark and I talk about peculiar things, like sheep, coyotes, teachers, countries, dogs, rabbits, etc. Just something to talk about so we won't have to say goodnight so soon, I guess. Tonight was different. Should I or shouldn't I tell? Will you keep it to yourself? Not as a secret but as a sacred. I had expected it, yet I hadn't. It was nice, but different. What? You ask what was it?

My first kiss.

We had walked to the door. He put his arm at my waist. We stood there, then he asked, "Well, aren't you going to kiss me goodnight?" So softly I said I guessed I would. I took a step toward his shoulder. It felt a bit of whiskers. All boys that are men enough have a few. It was a light kiss. One that was just barely a brush, you might say, but it was sweet. Mine on the right side of the lips. His on the right side of the lips. So a kiss is like this, I thought, and said "good night" once more, and we parted.

I do like him so.

June 19th, 1955 - Dear Diary, somehow it was different going to Orderville again. Oh! I had better come out of this after all. We three had another discussion. I can't keep things from them.

June 20th, 1955 - Dear Diary, guess who Wendy and I went with again? Yes, Guard and Donald. We didn't make it to leadership. We saw the show "Knights of the Round Table" and ate a lunch.

June 21st, 1955 - Dear Diary, I am really getting my share of nights out. I went to a M.I.A. party in the canyon where we had the Elder's party. I like that place.

June 22nd, 1955 - Dear Diary, I will have to watch what I write as well as what I say. Ikie causes a lot of trouble.

June 23rd, 1955 - Dear Diary, I am helping with the fruit stand. It isn't making any money yet. It is rather discouraging at times.

June 24th, 1955 - Dear Diary, Mama is sicker lately. She doesn't ever seem to get better.

June 25th, 1955 - Dear Diary, I cleaned up the yards today. Mark and I went to "City of Bad Men." His sister, Jessie, is working at the Y. We got her after work.

June 26th, 1955 - Dear Diary, we are all home once again. Everyone went to church. We three went to fireside. Mrs. Woodberry talked to us. It was very good.

June 27th, 1955 - Dear Diary, I sent Mark a birthday card and one of my Junior pictures. I bought the card when I was in Las Vegas.

June 28th, 1955 - Dear Diary, we are having a bad time with our M.I.A. young men. They have no teachers, so they will not come to M.I.A.

June 29th, 1955 - Dear Diary, tonight I went to town to see Aunt Arvilla about fair advertising. Last night was M.I.A. The night before was a fair meeting and a 4-H meeting.

June 30th, 1955 - Dear Diary, I have been trying to make a dress from two patterns and our imagination.

July 1st, 1955 - Dear Diary, it seemed good to go to a dance with Mark again. It seemed like it had been a long time since April. I don't know how he feels about Donald.

July 2nd, 1955 - Dear Diary, I stayed home tonight and tended kids while Mama and Daddy went to a party and Wendy went to a Kanab dance.

July 3rd, 1955 - Dear Diary, it has been a good Sunday. I have studied and heard about the Indians all day. In meeting, some talked. I read an article at fireside. Mrs. Dale talked.

July 4th, 1955 - Dear Diary, I went with Donald. He has a new car. We went to "Student Prince," ate a dinner, and went to the dance. I drove home again.

July 5th, 1955 - Dear Diary, we went to M.I.A. and played ball and roller skated. Wendy, Luanne, Sandra, and I really had fun. I got out of my ornery mood.

July 6th, 1955 - Dear Diary, I helped Aunt Eva wash today. Tonight I wrote a poem about, well guess? I can't help liking him better.

To A Dear Friend

My dear friend, I need to send to you
A poem expressing the feelings between us two.

Others say it's things in common to share.
I call it an understanding, knowing we care.

Care for each other and what is needed,
Are able to comfort and lift; so the call's heeded.

We know each other's joy and depression.
We inspire each other's thinking and talent's expression.

So it seems to me. You help me so.
Your writings and thoughts help me grow.

My dear friend, I need to send to you
This poem, saying: Friendship is love that's true.

July 7th, 1955 - Dear Diary, I helped tend the fruit stand today while Wendy had a 4-H meeting.

July 8th, 1955 - Dear Diary, I went with Mark tonight to "Broken Lance." It was a good show. LaVerl went with us. I didn't mind.

July 9th, 1955 - Dear Diary, we the family went to "Iuo Vadus." It was really a good show. It was good to all be together.

July 10th, 1955 - Dear Diary, we are all home once again. Weekends are good to have. Meeting was very good.

July 11th, 1955 - Dear Diary, Rita is staying with us for a while. We three girls went on dates to "Rose Marie" with Donald, Guard, and Duane.

July 12th, 1955 - Dear Diary, another party! M.I.A. this time. It was in the same place as before (as the Elder's party). There was a big crowd. It was fun.

July 13th, 1955 - Dear Diary, Rita and I climbed to Minchee and ate a lunch. We went wading. We went swimming in Lydie's. We climbed to Eagle Rock.

July 14th, 1955 - Dear Diary, Rita and I went with Phyllis to Alton. She is engaged. Rita went home this afternoon.

July 15th, 1955 - Dear Diary, Wendy and I went to Kanab this afternoon to get patterns and cloth. We had a fun afternoon.

July 16th, 1955 - Dear Diary, tonight Guard came to ask us to go to the show. Wendy said she would be busy. I said I thought I would have a date already. I haven't had one tonight however!

July 17th, 1955 - Dear Diary, we all went to church today. I tended kids and did the work while Mama, Daddy, and Wendy went to meeting.

July 18th, 1955 - Dear Diary, Wendy and I went to leadership. Who with? Guess. Yes. It was a dilly time but meeting was good and educational.

July 19th, 1955 - Dear Diary, we had another party (Jr. Gleaners and M. Men). It was up at the school house. Donald is in charge of the M. Men. Ramona in charge of Jr. Gleaners.

July 20th, 1955 - Dear Diary, Helen Jackson came to see me. We had a good visit. Wendy went to Cedar and got us both some 4-H cloth.

July 21st, 1955 - Dear Diary, we made an M.I.A. float for the parade. About nine of us were there.

July 22nd, 1955 - Dear Diary, the dance was a lot of fun. I danced a lot (for a change). Kenneth and Jeremy and two friends are here. Mark wasn't there.

July 23rd, 1955 - Dear Diary, today was the program (I sang) and the sports (they were a lot of fun). Us kids went on a crazy ride up the canyon. I went to a campfire program. No Mark.

July 24th, 1955 - Dear Diary, almost everyone was late sometime, somewhere today, and we all appear tired. But yesterday's and Friday's celebrations were something to remember.

July 25th, 1955 - Dear Diary, I went with Mark (and his family, I like them) to the show in Kanab, "White Feather."

July 26th, 1955 - Dear Diary, I helped make a broadcast today in Kanab. We are working to get ready for our 4-H trip. Mama and Daddy went to Cedar.

July 27th, 1955 - Dear Diary, we reached Duck Creek in time for breakfast. I am the secretary. I will have work to do. I am helping Wendy with her group.

July 28th, 1955 - Dear Diary, it is fun helping with a 4-H class. Helen J. and I went to Ice Cave this afternoon. Amy and I entered the log sawing.

July 29th, 1955 - Dear Diary, I really took notes at the awards meeting this morning. I was given some reed for my work.

July 30th, 1955 - Dear Diary, boy, am I sun burned and tired! I wrote 20 letters tonight, then went to bed. Wendy could have had three dates.

July 31st, 1955 - Dear Diary, we all went to church today. Mr. Fisher and Berk talked in meeting. We three went to fireside in Mt. Carmel.

August 1st, 1955 - Dear Diary, I haven't been feeling at all well today. I have had too much of something. Probably mix up.

August 2nd, 1955 - Dear Diary, I went to Kanab again to help make a report., even if I didn't feel like it. I didn't go to M.I.A.

August 3rd, 1955 - Dear Diary, I went to 4-H with Wendy to see about some fair business. I act as a reporter for the paper.

August 4th, 1955 - Dear Diary, between fair advertising, 4-H sewing, F.H.A. exhibits, M.I.A. chorister, and primary leading (once), I am busy.

August 5th, 1955 - Dear Diary, I am sewing a lot lately on a red corduroy suit. I walked home from Glendale (from business articles I wrote).

August 6th, 1955 - Dear Diary, Mama and I convinced Daddy to take us to the show "Give a Girl a Break." It was really good.

August 7th, 1955 - Dear Diary, I lead the singing (for Elaine) in the Primary Conference tonight. It was really fun!

August 8th, 1955 - Dear Diary, I went to another fair and 4-H meeting tonight. I rode down with Tom and Wendy. I came home with Philip.

August 9th, 1955 - Dear Diary, Mama went to Cedar today to get some teeth out. She is staying at Jean's tonight.

August 10th, 1955 - Dear Diary, I am glad Mama came home today. We had a fun party at the lake (Natalie and Logan's). Wendy was with Dean.

August 11th, 1955 - Dear Diary, I am to sing tomorrow night. So I practiced with Amy today. Mama bought me some music for the talent contest. I walked home and of course sewed today.

August 12th, 1955 - Dear Diary, Wendy and I went to Kanab to an M.I.A. stake dance. It was very fun. I haven't had so much fun! I sang "A Dream is a Wish your Heart Makes." No Mark.

August 13th, 1955 - Dear Diary, Rita is in the hospital for appendicitis. I went to an Elder's dance in Alton with Mark. It was not as fun as last night. Oh dear!

August 14th, 1955 - Dear Diary, I stayed at Luanne's today to practice a song we are to sing in conference next Sunday.

August 15th, 1955 - Dear Diary, Wendy and I went to town for practicing and 4-H. Tonight, she and I went with Donald to leadership in Fredonia. We had fun.

August 16th, 1955 - Dear Diary, I stayed in the fruit stand today then went practicing and to M.I.A. We had a wonderful meeting.

August 17th, 1955 - Dear Diary, every day I try to practice my songs and sew. Today I sang for two hours. I got too engrossed.

August 18th, 1955 - Dear Diary, I didn't get to practice today at all. Mama is having a bad time with her teeth, and I am doing the work.

August 19th, 1955 - Dear Diary, Wendy, Lincoln, and I went to Kanab's dance with Robert Tally from Philadelphia, Pennsylvania. He really is quite a guy!

August 20th, 1955 - Dear Diary, tonight I went to the dance in Kanab with Dale Parks. Wendy goes with his brother, Thomas Parks. I really like them.

August 21st, 1955 - Dear Diary, conference was very good. Adam S. Bennion is wonderful. Luanne Easton and I sang "O Divine Redeemer" in M.I.A. meeting.

August 22nd, 1955 - Dear Diary, I went to "A Man Called Peter" with Donald. Wendy and Tom were there too. Oh, Thomas Parks!!

August 23rd, 1955 - Dear Diary, it is raining tonight, and I have caught cold, so no one is going to M.I.A. Wendy and I have sewing to get done for the fair. I helped Aunt Eva wash, and they had dinner at our place. Ike came from Salt Lake.

August 24th, 1955 - Dear Diary, our days are full of fair business, the fruit stand, the house, and all, but sewing and caring for a sore throat is neglected.

August 25th, 1955 - Dear Diary, time goes by so very fast! Our suits, blue wool and red corduroy, are almost finished. I can't seem to get rid of this cold!

August 26th, 1955 - Dear Diary, we were all so thrilled tonight! Wendy was crowned "Miss Kane County." Oh, for thrilling! A wonderful night.

August 27th, 1955 - Dear Diary, I sang "Because" in the talent show (in the new gym). I won the vocal trophy! It is all worth it. It seemed like some wonderful dream. No Mark, and I didn't care!

August 28th, 1955 - Dear Diary, it has seemed so good today to have nothing that is urgent to be done and to just rest for a change and not worry about a thing.

Dear Diary, this month of August has been most wonderful! Why? Well, it has for a number of reasons. I don't remember ever being so busy. It has been eventful. Some events were just what I have dreamed of and wanted.

It was thrilling to lead primary kids in singing.

I think most of it started (really) on the night of the 12th. I sang at the M.I.A. dance in Kanab. I danced too. Oh, it was fun. I hardly sat out a dance. Tom began it. I have never liked dancing more. He dances – Oh, how can I express it? Like a dream – a smooth exciting dream I have found worth waiting for. But - what am I saying! He likes Wendy. I have her to thank for this chance of dancing with and even of seeing Tom. And I can't get his face, his eyes, out of my mind.

I had better get on with events and not write too much of some things.

Bob Tally is quite a guy. He met Wendy at the fruit stand and decided to come back. There was another fun dance at Kanab, open-air (thanks to Bob and his car). I met my date for August 20th.

Wendy and Tom did some arranging for younger brother and sister. It worked just right! I had a date with Dale Parks. We had never seen each other until the night before our date. Exciting? Yes! As Wendy, Bob, Lincoln, and I went to the dance pavilion, we saw the two brothers sitting, no standing, together. It was quite dark. They looked just alike!

Boy, I was glad. This was better than I had expected! I knew Dale was wondering. So was I. Tom danced with me and said he would introduce us, and he did. Dale isn't just like Tom, in fact he is really different, but still I like him. He was said to be shy, not a good dancer, an artist, very studious, smart, and quite anti-social. Tom is not shy, is a wonderful dancer, also an artist, quite smart, and social. I like them both. It seemed easier to talk to Dale.

Our dates were a lot of fun

The next day was conference. It was an exceptionally good conference! That evening Luanne and I sang in M.I.A. conference. Tom was there but Dale wasn't. Wendy had a date with Derryl Heaton. Lincoln and I went along. All of the Kanab boys were in competition for Wendy. I got to feeling like a tag along. It wasn't so bad going home, though I goofed some. Landel was with Deryll too. We all sang as we rode home in the convertible.

The fair was something I can't forget. We entered our things and got in on the parade. I saw there were ten pictures of Dale's and one of Tom's. They are artists.

That night was thrilling for all of us. Oh, we were proud and happy! Wendy was crowned "Miss Kane County." She really was popular then.

I danced with Lincoln, Kenneth, Donald, Mark, I think a few others, and Tom (Tom before Mark). He was proud too. The Monday before, Wendy thought, would result in Tom's absence. She may wonder if there is an understanding. It was quite a talk they had that Monday night after "A Man Called Peter." I had had a date too (Donald).

The last night of the fair was the grandest for me. I sang "Because" in the talent show. First, I danced with Paul, then Jeremy, Orton, and Lincoln. I was called to the stage. I had won the vocal trophy. Gosh, I was happy all night. So many were glad! I danced afterward, first with Laundel (remember L.J.H.), then Derryl, Lincoln, Karry, and Tom (who I think is having rebound trouble), then Donald. Mark was not there, but somehow I didn't miss him or feel bad. It is best this way too. As I think of all of the fun, the exciting events of the fair, I wonder if it all is but a dream that has to end. That last fair day I saw and talked to Dale when he came to see his painting. I was glad to see him and tell him how I liked his pictures.

I wonder what will happen in the future as a result of this August and its events. It has fulfilled things for me. So many of those dreams and expectations! Will it continue on or must I realize I am to ease myself down, down from a rosy cloud – that is dancing smoothly, dreamingly, holding a shine of wishes come true?

August 29th, 1955 - Dear Diary, oh, who wants to get back into old routines again? It is hard to come back from everything.

August 30th, 1955 - Dear Diary, we did not get to M.I.A. tonight because of the car, so I drew and painted a picture. I have been needing to.

August 31st, 1955 - Dear Diary, so ends this grand August, with a lone walk in the moonlight to settle, in the heart, events and feelings.

September 1st, 1955 - Dear Diary, I went to Kanab today and bought some cloth for two skirts and blouses for school.

September 2nd, 1955 - Dear Diary, we three made a cake for Mama. Aunt Eva came to supper. I and the kids put on a play in the barn.

September 3rd, 1955 - Dear Diary, I am now at Glendale, staying with Karen, Ora May, and Sherman while the folks are at Hole in the Rock. It has been a job today.

September 4th, 1955 - Dear Diary, I gave a talk in Sunday school in Orderville. Norma and I took all of the kids (six of her siblings and three of mine) to church at noon.

September 5th, 1955 - Dear Diary, we have all been sewing. I am trying to finish a dress for school. Aunt Eva and Uncle Neldon came this evening.

September 6th, 1955 - Dear Diary, we began school today. We will have a new music teacher and principal (we don't know him yet). We Seniors had a party at Navajo. It is one I shall always remember!

September 7th, 1955 - Dear Diary, today we registered all over again. We still have no definite principal. We were out at noon.

September 8th, 1955 - Dear Diary, my hair in shorter now and curly. I had a permanent. I am confused about the art class I want to take, along with Music Appreciation by Mr. Fox.

September 9th, 1955 - Dear Diary, I am getting lonesome for "another" dance again so soon. But would any other dance be like August's? I am still having dreams, I guess.

September 10th, 1955 - Dear Diary, I helped serve at a banquet tonight. It was some experience! We got in on some eats too. Donald brought me home.

September 11th, 1955 - Dear Diary, we all went to Sunday School, but the car has no lights now, so only part of us went to meeting.

September 12th, 1955 - Dear Diary, we have another new teacher. Mr. Farson is going to be a good teacher, we all think. He teaches Am. Prob.

September 13th, 1955 - Dear Diary, I stayed down at Rita's tonight so I could go to M.I.A., and I sang "An Angel From on High." I led the singing.

September 14th, 1955 - Dear Diary, I am taking Art instead of Music Appreciation. It is too much beyond me and my interest. Mr. Fox won't mind. My folks might.

September 15th, 1955 - Dear Diary, the two morning classes have been changed. All classes may be changed again.

September 16th, 1955 - Dear Diary, we had a school party tonight. There really is a group in high school, Rita and I decided.

September 17th, 1955 - Dear Diary, I went with Donald to "Captain Lightfoot" and the Kanab dance. Thomas and Wendy were there. I danced with Tom. He leaves tomorrow to go to University of Utah.

September 18th, 1955 - Dear Diary, it is hard to believe Grandma is dead and will not be in St. George. As it seems, it happened so suddenly.

September 19th, 1955 - Dear Diary, Daddy is in St. George or Cedar. All of Grandma's children are coming home. Uncle Alma is coming from Japan, Laska and Cram from Colorado.

September 20th, 1955 - Dear Diary, Wendy left for the State Fair. Mama, Ike, and I went with Donald to M.I.A. A new boy, Phil B., came to Mutual.

September 21st, 1955 - Dear Diary, the funeral has been postponed twice. It shall be tomorrow in order to have everyone there.

September 22nd, 1955 - Dear Diary, the funeral services were very nice. We went to both. Mama went up to Salt Lake.

September 23rd, 1955 - Dear Diary, I did not go to the dance tonight. Daddy just got home. He brought some things from Grandma.

September 24th, 1955 - Dear Diary, taking care of our family has just about got me down!

September 25th, 1955 - Dear Diary, Mama and Wendy got home this afternoon. Wendy had to get packed and leave soon after for Cedar and college.

September 26th, 1955 - Dear Diary, some new boys came to Sunday school and school. They are Craig, Cloyd, and Leoran.

September 27th, 1955 - Dear Diary, I took charge of the Mia Maids' "Sing a Lesson" tonight. I helped them learn some songs (I hope they learned). Mr. Fox gave Luanne and me a music book to study.

September 28th, 1955 - Dear Diary, this year, Typing is going to be my hardest class. It seems, however, this year's studies aren't going to be very hard.

September 29th, 1955 - Dear Diary, I didn't go to the F.H.A./F.F.A. party tonight. I stayed home and cut out a blouse and tended kids.

September 30th, 1955 - Dear Diary, I went to the Freshie Frolic and another Sr. party! We have really given an initiation to those Freshmen.

October 1st, 1955 - Dear Diary, Wendy came home for the weekend. She is enthused about college. Sometimes I wish I were there too.

October 2nd, 1955 - Dear Diary, we are all home, once again. For Lincoln's birthday (on Oct. 4th), we had a family party, all ten of us, then Wendy left, and Lincoln will be leaving. He talked in meeting.

October 3rd, 1955 - Dear Diary, Luanne and I are going to take music lessons together! I am also enjoying Jenny's and my art class. Am. Pro. is interesting. Craig seems to be quite a guy. I believe he sings.

October 4th, 1955 - Dear Diary, I didn't get to M.I.A. tonight, and I really should have! Lincoln is 20, and just think, old enough to go on a mission.

October 5th, 1955 - Dear Diary, all of the Senior girls but two, one was me, went to Cedar tonight to a show. I have been doing too much.

October 6th, 1955 - Dear Diary, some of us kids went up Lydie's Canyon and had a wiener roast, and I made a cake. We had fun!

October 7th, 1955 - Dear Diary, I went with Lincoln to Elaine and Gene's wedding dance. I came home with Mark, Jenny, Rita, Jinks, and Steven. I can't feel the way I used to. I kept thinking of August, etc. (or just Tom).

October 8th, 1955 - Dear Diary, we had a big banquet at Orderville tonight. We all went and had a good time.

October 9th, 1955 - Dear Diary, they have asked me to teach a Sunday school class. I surely hope I can do it right.

October 10th, 1955 - Dear Diary, we had a Seminary party tonight. It was a good one too! I wrote Wendy a letter (a problem one). I can't seem to forget him, and he can't know it.

October 11th, 1955 - Dear Diary, I stayed down to M.I.A. tonight, so I could type for a while. We beat Kanab in baseball!

October 12th, 1955 - Dear Diary, we were out early for U.E.A. The F.H.A. had the sleeping party and initiation tonight in the new gym.

October 13th, 1955 - Dear Diary, I came home this morning mighty tired. It was fun anyway! Lincoln and Craig are going over the mountain. Leorin is here.

October 14th, 1955 - Dear Diary, things seem so lonesome every once in a while. But I can't write letters to everybody. I will care for four. She won't mind. He won't know.

October 15th, 1955 - Dear Diary, we got a terrible scare today! Rumor said Wendy was killed in a car wreck. It isn't at all true, thank goodness. Lincoln, Craig, and I went to Arrowhead and Virginia and Johnny's reception.

October 16th, 1955 - Dear Diary, I taught my Sunday school class today. Claude was with Ikie today. I feel so lonesome tonight (weekend blues or something). 300 miles and no chance. I feel I love one I have never gone with.

October 17th, 1955 - Dear Diary, guess what! Arlene is engaged to Larsen. I am happy for them. Oh, Arlene!

October 18th, 1955 - Dear Diary, tonight in M.I.A. we had a Jr. Gleaner Comradery at Lorine's.

October 19th, 1955 - Dear Diary, I finally got a letter from Wendy. She is really fitting in to college life. She advises me to enjoy school.

October 20th, 1955 - Dear Diary, we are having yearbook pictures taken today and tomorrow.

October 21st, 1955 - Dear Diary, finally, they are all taken. I feel I am going to be sick for a while.

October 22nd, 1955 - Dear Diary, Lincoln, Craig, and Daddy went hunting. I went to the doctor today and got three bottles of pills.

October 23rd, 1955 - Dear Diary, boy, does my throat (mouth) hurt. I have been in bed all day. I can't eat.

October 24th, 1955 - Dear Diary, the Errings are here again (and I sick again). I am reading "The Eagle's Song," "The Real Man," "Amaranth," "Dream Life," "Best Loved Stories," and two literature books. Rose and Rita came to see me.

October 26th, 1955 - Dear Diary, I am beginning to wonder when I will be well again. I can't seem to find any cure. Craig is having a party tonight at his place. I would like to have gone.

October 27th, 1955 - Dear Diary, there is lots of time to think and dream, lying here in bed. I wonder how many (if any) will come true. I went to Kanab again. I now have a purple mouth, throat, lips, and teeth.

Dear Diary, I might just as well write a minute. I am sure I have time. Yes, I'm still sick. I can't seem to get better. There is something wrong with my mouth. I might go to the doctor again.

It is pretty outside, but it is getting colder all of the time.

Dear Diary, this year seems so different. There are new teachers, new building, and it seems, too big of a loss of students. There seems to be a tendency to get the blues and lonesomeness, wishing we were some other place. I believe about the most wonderful thing this year is a new unity among our class. Each one seems to mean more now. Why? Probably because we have had to work and pull together. Maybe it is because we are beginning to realize this is our last year together, a time to sum up things and make them really count. I find all of the girls are sweet and willing to do all they can to help. In spite of all of the things I may have said about a classmate (when I was mad or jealous), I want it understood I really do love each of them. This last year (of school) I should do all I can to prove it.

Dear Diary, I often find myself giving advice and understanding to those who are blue. Maybe I should use some for myself.

What is a year or two or three compared to a lifetime and eternity?

He will come back – things will work out, if he is the right one.

We like someone because,

We love them although,

Love sought is good, but given unsought is better.

October 28th, 1955 - Dear Diary, so again, I don't get to go to the dance. I am out of bed and well enough to write Wendy a letter. We got a new car today. Mike had a party.

October 29th, 1955 - Dear Diary, I cleaned the upstairs. Aunt Helen, Rua, Stan, and Iver have been here these two days. Craig and Lincoln went hunting again.

October 30th , 1955 - Dear Diary, I must be getting better. I did a big batch of dishes. But oh, this dark purple looks a sight!

October 31st, 1955 - Dear Diary, I'm omitting the purple and seeing if I can some way find a cure. Bishops had another party tonight, and I didn't get to go again.

My Dearest Diary

November 1st, 1955 - Dear Diary, it has hurt so much today. I'm about to wonder if it is incurable. Daddy bought me two new medicines. I'll try anything. After this, I had better never feel sorry.

November 2nd, 1955 - Dear Diary, I am going to school tomorrow, if possible. I feel somewhat better. Mr. Henderson came to ask me about the play. I had better continue to get better and fast.

November 3rd, 1955 - Dear Diary, I stayed down to play practice tonight. Yes – I went to school today. I'm so glad to be well again.

November 4th, 1955 - Dear Diary, I went (alone) to the dance tonight. It left a few mixed up feelings, in more minds than one.

November 5th, 1955 - Dear Diary, I have stayed home and taken care of the family while Mama went to Cedar to get her teeth.

November 6th, 1955 - Dear Diary, conference was really wonderful today and tonight. Mr. Brown and Mr. Love were down (current bush, trials, and prayer).

November 7th, 1955 - Dear Diary, I stayed down and typed until about 6:30 then went to Rita's until 7:30, then we had play practice until 10:30. Went to bed about 11:30.

November 8th, 1955 - Dear Diary, oh, it seems so good to be doing things again. I went to practice tonight, made signs, and waited with the boys and Craig for Daddy.

November 9th, 1955 - Dear Diary, we did our play today and tonight. It was rather scary and a little goofed.

November 10th, 1955 - Dear Diary, oh, what times to remember! We put on the play again. It went better this time. Then we all had a party.

November 11th, 1955 - Dear Diary, the play "They Gave Him a Co-ed" was fun putting on. I will always remember it!

November 12th, 1955 - Dear Diary, goodness, I am tired. This week has really been busy and fun.

November 13th, 1955 - Dear Diary, I went to church today. It seemed so good. I taught my class. Larry M. was one of the speakers in meeting. Mr. and Mrs. Bishop talked in fireside.

November 14th, 1955 - Dear Diary, we awoke to snow this morning. It seems so sudden. Winter is not far off.

November 15th, 1955 - Dear Diary, I went to M.I.A. It's about time. Ramona wasn't there. She is hurt. We danced and had a lesson.

November 16th, 1955 - Dear Diary, oh, I need a typewriter. I am still behind and having a heck of a time. I am writing a play.

November 17th, 1955 - Dear Diary, today the pictures came. Luanne and I had a first lesson tonight. I learned something besides music. I went to a 4-H meeting. We took aptitude tests.

November 18th, 1955 - Dear Diary, our Senior Hop was a lot of fun, I thought (it was formal). Our theme is "Love is a Many Splendored Thing." We had an early party afterwards (3:00 o'clock).

November 19th, 1955 - Dear Diary, I'm so darn tired today. 3:00 is too early. I don't see how Craig and Lincoln can stay hunting so long. I have also caught cold.

November 20th, 1955 - Dear Diary, I have been home all day trying to recuperate. It makes me mad. I missed a lot. Thomas and Dale's mother talked in meeting.

November 21st, 1955 - Dear Diary, our F.H.A. had a program tonight. We officers wore our formals. It was inspiring and fun.

November 22nd, 1955 - Dear Diary, tonight was the ward speech festival. Lincoln, Luanne, Elaine, and Mr. Fawson talked. Elaine won. Luanne and I had another lesson.

November 23rd, 1955 - Dear Diary, we had an assembly and dance today. Craig and I both sang solos, "It is no Secret" and "I Need You Now" and "Because." Craig can really sing!

November 24th, 1955 - Dear Diary, we had a wonderful Thanksgiving. Aunt Eva's family and our family went to St. George to Grandpa and Becca's.

November 25th, 1955 - Dear Diary, it seems so good to all be home, but I'm ornery tonight. Wendy got a date to the play, and I didn't. She went with Jim in Mark's new car. He also had a date.

November 26th, 1955 - Dear Diary, the night I have waited 70 days for came. Most of us went to "Gone with the Wind." Then Lincoln, Wendy, and I came home and got ready for the Gold and Green Ball. We got there for the last few minutes. It was worth it. Wendy and I found we were the only ones who wore formals. Well, it didn't matter.

Lincoln and Wendy started dancing. I danced with Paul. Wendy danced with (yes, he and Dale did come) Thomas. I danced with Thomas. Wendy danced with Dale. It ended (Thomas traded) with Wendy dancing with Thomas and me dancing with Dale.

It seemed so good to see him (whether he would acknowledge it or not).

I like Dale too.

If things (and people) don't change, I could go on feeling like this for years and more.

Thomas Parks
Tom, Tom, Tom
Thomas
Mr. Thomas Parks
Mrs. Thomas Parks
Thomas Parks and family
What a dream. Wake up? (for someone) who??

November 27th, 1955 - Dear Diary, Wendy went back. Church was good. I taught my class. Lincoln, Craig, and I went to fireside. Craig says he and I are buddies. I would like to adopt him for a brother.

Dear Diary, there is nobody quite like Craig.

With Wendy and Lincoln soon both to be gone, I would sure like to adopt him for a brother. We get along so well. He tells me of his girlfriend, ambitions, and everything, just like Lincoln does. I hope LaTrese, "Trese," appreciates him. Everyone seems to think he is wonderful. He is, but they don't know like I do. I really would like him for a brother (understand?). I hope when Lincoln leaves, he doesn't too.

November 28th, 1955 - Dear Diary, I handed in my play, "The Sign is Given," for the Seminary contest. I'm afraid I am not working hard enough. School seems too easy (all but Typing).

November 29th, 1955 - Dear Diary, Mama and I went to Kanab tonight to a "Sacred to Me" meeting. It was a night to remember. Mrs. Wight talked to us. It was in Kanab's new elementary building. I sang "My Friend."

November 30th, 1955 - Dear Diary, we saw a show today, "The High and the Mighty." Mr. Conover came, and we planned more for the yearbooks.

December 1st, 1955 - Dear Diary, I am playing cupid for Craig and LaTrese. Something is bound to happen! Craig wanted me to write a letter, so I did.

December 2nd, 1955 - Dear Diary, tonight we played Marysville in Kanab's new gym (everyone is jealous of Kanab). I hope they change. We were beat.

December 3rd, 1955 - Dear Diary, I have cleaned house all day. Tonight I found an article to keep. It is about someone (Darnell) I admire, "Dedication of a Youth to a Cause."

December 4th, 1955 - Dear Diary, I love teaching my Sunday school class. Daddy and Mama and I went to meeting tonight. We all went to testament meeting. Then Mama and I spent an interesting few hours at Aunt Maime and Uncle Ed's.

December 5th, 1955 - Dear Diary, I got the highest score in Seminary on a test, and Amy and I got the highest in Am. Prob. But then along comes Typing with a C. Woe is me.

December 6th, 1955 - Dear Diary, I had a good time tonight, even if I didn't get to go to a party with Luanne. I will always remember tonight.

December 7th, 1955 - Dear Diary, Jenny has been to California. We have been having yearbook troubles.

December 8th, 1955 - Dear Diary, I have been playing cupid, as I said. And something did happen. I got a letter. I think I'm going to like LaTrese.

December 9th, 1955 - Dear Diary, Arlene, Rita, Lincoln, and I went with Craig to Kanab to the game. We didn't win, but it was still a fun night.

December 10th, 1955 - Dear Diary, I stayed home today and worked as usual. Mama is sewing for Mary Ann.

December 11th, 1955 - Dear Diary, I taught my class today. I went to one and a half meetings and a fireside. I went to Kanab with LeAnn.

December 12th, 1955 - Dear Diary, my play was one that was chosen (many weren't entered). Now for the production! We lost another game.

December 13th, 1955 - Dear Diary, we have the phones in now, but they are not all regulated. We had fun dancing in M.I.A. tonight.

December 14th, 1955 - Dear Diary, this play is going to be fun!! Just think, it is my very own "first production!!"

December 16th, 1955 - Dear Diary, Rita asked me to go to a show with her, but I decided not to. Today, Kanab presented their exchange assembly. It was very good.

December 17th, 1955 - Dear Diary, today there was a temple excursion. Lincoln got his endowments, so did Darnell (and he is only 19). I think it's wonderful!

December 18th, 1955 - Dear Diary, I went to Cedar today to "The Messiah." I liked it. I saw Wendy for a few minutes.

December 19th, 1955 - Dear Diary, Arlene doesn't want to get married. I guess the engagement is off. I feel sorry for Larson.

December 20th, 1955 - Dear Diary, the M.I.A. party was fun. Some of us girls got on a crazy streak and acted just like we felt.

December 21st, 1955 - Dear Diary, I am so busy trying to do Seminary, Yearbook, Chorus, etc., my mind gets in a flurry.

December 22nd, 1955 - Dear Diary, tonight "The Sign Is Given" was presented. This is a time to always remember.

December 23rd, 1955 - Dear Diary, the play is over. The yearbook section is sent in. Oh, happy day!

December 24th, 1955 - Dear Diary, it is Christmas Eve already! Wendy came home. We went to a program. I met Keith Bishop and sang, and we had a party for Lincoln.

December 25th, 1955 - Dear Diary, these last few days are to be cherished. We are all home now. It will be for the last time in years. It seems so good.

December 26th, 1955 - Dear Diary, Wendy went back to Cedar. The rest of us went to the dance with three basket lunches. Donald bid the highest (twice) for mine. It was quite a night.

December 27th, 1955 - Dear Diary, what a sad mixed up muddle! I've got to stop building bridges. I just haven't understood enough. I went to a dance in Kanab with Donald. Yes, I knew Tom would be there.

December 28th, 1955 - Dear Diary, I went to a ballgame tonight and sold candy for the yearbook. I went to Dee's farewell party. It was really nice.

December 29th, 1955 - Dear Diary, I'm afraid I'm having remorse of conscience. It hurts to hurt other people. You know, maybe I don't deserve who I want. I went to another ballgame.

December 30th, 1955 - Dear Diary, tonight is a night I shall never forget. We had Lincoln's farewell program and dance in the old Valley gym. There was a large crowd. Grandpa and Becca came.

All of the folks were there. Wendy and Janice came over with Gary. Wendy advised me to note Thomas also came.

The dance began with square dancing, then regular dancing to records.

In the middle of the dance, about six cakes were auctioned off for $92.00. Mr. LeFever came. Craig and I started the program. We sang, "I Know that my Redeemer Lives." Elaine gave a reading. Mr. LaFever talked. It was really good. Lincoln thanked everyone and said he would do his best. We were so proud of him! I'm glad everything was so wonderful for him. What a night to remember and cherish.

When I was dancing with Craig, we decided that since we both would be so in need, to adopt each other. Now he is my brother, and I am his "Sis." It makes us feel better.

A lot of people told us they liked our song. One time, Tom put his hand on my shoulder. He had to, to get my attention (sometimes I act so queer) and looked at me.

"That was wonderful," he said. And I believe he really meant it. He must be learning to understand. He seems always to be changing, or growing better, in my opinion. I don't know his opinion of me. I can just try to make it a good one.

It was very nice of him to come to Lincoln's dance. Of course, he must have guessed Wendy was there. I admire the sense he has of manipulating. He must be quite sincere himself. Well, I had better stop talking about Thomas Parks and close for now.

December 31st, 1955 - Dear Diary, what a night! Guess what? I got to share a date with Thomas. I knew something would have to happen. This is a night I'll remember.

Dear Diary, Wendy went back to Cedar last night after the party. Tonight was the Senior project dance. I planned on going with Lincoln. He went to Cedar and was to bring Wendy home with him. I was planning for the dance around 8:00, when the phone rang. It was for Mama. Wendy had had a change of plans. She couldn't get home by 9:00 (and she had a date with Tom for that time). So guess what she did (what else could she have done)?

She told Mama to arrange for me to go with Tom to the dance, then she and Lincoln would meet us there after a while. Oh, talk about feelings! I didn't know if I could make it (I mean, oh, you know what I mean).

He was awfully nice about it. I couldn't help but admire him all the more. It wasn't as hard as I thought it would be. I enjoyed it whether he did or not. I will never forget this night. Like Tom said, "Things like this are what make life interesting." Tonight was an answer to me. He will have changed some of his understanding. I still feel the same.

Wendy and Lincoln came, after quite a while, and dates were exchanged. There was a party at Easton's afterwards. The night was, I would call, very extra ordinary indeed. Wouldn't you? One just never knows. Thomas, did I ruin a wonderful night for you? Just how much will you remember and understand?

Memorandum 1955

Dear Diary, 1955 has been a year of growing. It has witnessed much changing. There have been many things to treasure. I believe I am growing up or learning more about it.

1956

January 1st, 1956 - Dear Diary, we all went together to church today. This is to be our last Sunday together for years.

January 2nd, 1956 - Dear Diary, today more preparations were made for Lincoln's mission. We were all home.

January 3rd, 1956 - Dear Diary, Lincoln left for Salt Lake. Wendy left for Cedar. A family divided. We three "to go separate ways."

January 4th, 1956 - Dear Diary, school started again today. Have the past few days really happened? I am left with an empty feeling, but with memories also.

January 5th, 1956 - Dear Diary, we are putting on more plays. I am in one, "Dark Wind" (Dr. Fleming). So it's back to school again.

January 6th, 1956 - Dear Diary, I went to a game and a dance tonight. It all seemed so empty and sort of "unreal." Why, I had better come out of it!!

January 7th, 1956 - Dear Diary, I cleaned the house today and wrote a letter to Lincoln. It seems an age since he was here.

January 8th, 1956 - Dear Diary, I taught my class. Tonight I went to fireside with Craig. Thank goodness he's still here. Bless him!

January 9th, 1956 - Dear Diary, I have been awful tired all day today. My eyes seem to bother me. Craig says he's sleepy.

January 10th, 1956 - Dear Diary, we went to M.I.A. tonight (for a change). I hope we continue. I received $2.00 for "The Sign is Given." I bought a $2.00 billfold.

January 11th, 1956 - Dear Diary, Jenny and I are helping Eva paint a picture in the church house. It is interesting. Jenny and I both have letters from Lincoln.

January 12th, 1956 - Dear Diary, I feel so like I could be a "love lorn-ist." Isn't that what a love counselor is called? I am glad I have friends who confide in me.

January 13th, 1956 - Dear Diary, we played Kanab tonight. They beat us by two points! It was quite a game (quite a night)! Ask Rita, or Rose (a few dreams crushed).

January 14th, 1956 - Dear Diary, compare things with a year ago. Don't things change? Now, Mark is going on a mission to Holland. I went to his farewell. There is no said understanding.

January 15th, 1956 - Dear Diary, Wendy was here since Friday. Left again. We went to Kanab Saturday. I went to a preparation meeting today. Craig is still "up north."

January 16th, 1956 - Dear Diary, I am so lonesome again! Mark's leaving made me feel so odd. I can't explain all these feelings. I do so miss my other brother too. I went to a show and film.

January 17th, 1956 - Dear Diary, we danced for a few minutes in M.I.A., and then we had a short lesson. Both classes together.

January 18th, 1956 - Dear Diary, we had a test in Seminary today. We have finished the "Book of Mormon."

January 19th, 1956 - Dear Diary, the last of the yearbook pictures are to be taken tomorrow. It will seem good to finally get them all over with.

January 20th, 1956 - Dear Diary, well, I am 18. It hasn't seemed like a birthday. I have been busy with yearbook, and no one remembered, but Rita and Craig reminded Mama (accidentally).

January 21st, 1956 - Dear Diary, since the family forgot my birthday yesterday, tonight we had a family party. I got a sweet card from Wendy.

January 22nd, 1956 - Dear Diary, I love my darling Sunday School class. Each one of them is so sweet.

January 23rd, 1956 - Dear Diary, we are going to study courtship and marriage in Seminary. It will really be interesting.

January 24th, 1956 - Dear Diary, we had a wonderful M.I.A. testimony class tonight. I feel happy! Craig is so admirable and fine (most of the time). Oh, brotherly love!

January 25th, 1956 - Dear Diary, we had a fun party tonight. I stayed down after school at Craig's to dance with Claude. Then we had a Sunday school party.

January 26th, 1956 - Dear Diary, Rita and I didn't get up very early today. I stayed at Bishops again and practiced. I didn't get home until late.

January 27th, 1956 - Dear Diary, Cedar did not come over tonight, so the game was called off. I spent a night home getting ready to go to St. George.

January 28th, 1956 - Dear Diary, I went to the temple today with Bishops. Three of us were baptized 35 times. I went to the Gold and Green Ball.

January 29th, 1956 - Dear Diary, I spent most of a day and night in town again. I went to Kanab for a practice.

January 30th, 1956 - Dear Diary, I'm sure tired. I had better be getting some sleep. I need to live home more often.

January 31st, 1956 - Dear Diary, we did the dance in an M.I.A. program. The guys looked nice in their Spanish costumes.

February 1st, 1956 - Dear Diary, today is Luanne's birthday. I gave her a card and handkerchief. She is so sweet.

February 2nd, 1956 - Dear Diary, we are trying to get the concert ready for Saturday. We have been getting out of an extra class.

February 3rd, 1956 - Dear Diary, we went to school for just a half a day today. The power was off last night. I didn't go to any classes.

February 4th, 1956 - Dear Diary, we had our concert tonight. I believe it was good too. I know it was thrilling and special.

February 5th, 1956 - Dear Diary, I went to conference today, thanks to manipulation. We came home with Bishops. Craig let me read his patriarchal blessing. It really is wonderful! He showed me more of his things and gave me some pictures of him, then came up home after milk. That means a good visit. I like them.

February 7th, 1956 - Dear Diary, we had a typing session after school. I stayed down and typed Craig's blessing for him. It took from 3:30 to 6:00 (M.I.A. at 5:00). We went home and had supper.

February 8th, 1956 - Dear Diary, I stayed home tonight and made valentines. I am making about 22 to send to some friends and loved ones.

February 9th, 1956 - Dear Diary, today Cedar (C.S.U.) brought over an assembly. It was really good. I wish I could have talked to Chad T.

February 10th, 1956 - Dear Diary, Claude asked me to stay to dancing. Afterwards, we did dishes, and Craig made candy. They brought me home. I went back and sang in P.T.A. (in a double trio).

February 11th, 1956 - Dear Diary, I did a lot of house cleaning today. Remember how things were at this time last year? My how things change!

February 12th, 1956 - Dear Diary, tonight Craig talked in church. He talked about "friends." He and I went to fireside at Rita's.

February 13th, 1956 - Dear Diary, I went to an F.H.A. party tonight. I was up until 1:00 finishing valentines to put in lockers tomorrow.

February 14th, 1956 - Dear Diary, it has been quite a Valentine's Day. Guess what! Craig (and probably the others) gave me a box of candy. I went to M.I.A. with them. Craig and I sang.
    Dear Diary, what a night! I delivered valentines at Bishops. They had me stay a while. The boys came home. They were ready

for M.I.A. Craig handed me a valentine of candy, "orange chocolate sticks." We four went to Mt. Carmel to the party. Craig and I sang "Reuben and Rachael." I had fun dancing. He brought me home. He needed some milk and butter. He stayed until 11:00. I opened the candy. Oh, what times to remember!

Dear Diary, I am so thankful for my other brothers. They treat me so nice. Without them, I don't know how it would be, probably awful lonesome.

One may wish for things she thinks she wants. How much better off she is when she knows the things she has she both wants and needs.

I love my adopted family.

February 15th, 1956 - Dear Diary, we played Kanab. In the last minute and a half, they beat us by two points. Oh!! Last Friday we had a time. Mr. Demille talked to us, and we all cried over our boys.

February 16th, 1956 - Dear Diary, today we had a social meeting with two men counselors. It was really good. We got our aptitude tests back. I still plan on Education at C.S.U.

February 17th, 1956 - Dear Diary, guess what! We won a basketball game, for once. We beat Enterprise by 20 points. Isn't that something! Claude and I had fun dancing.

February 18th, 1956 - Dear Diary, I did house work today, as usual. Remember last year at this time? Sometimes I miss those weekends.

February 19th, 1956 - Dear Diary, I sure love my Sunday School class, even if they are too little to understand (lessons). I stayed at Luanne's today.

February 20th, 1956 - Dear Diary, I sure don't do much in school this year. Most of my worries are extracurricular (you know – yearbook, etc.).

February 21st, 1956 - Dear Diary, I sure played a dumb one tonight!! Oh, don't let me slip. (Brother Craig) I must keep the adjective in mind.

February 22nd, 1956 - Dear Diary, I'm in a middle of a yearbook muddle. Arlene is sick. I don't know how we would make out without Jenny and Helen.

February 23rd, 1956 - Dear Diary, now that the yearbook section is in the mail, maybe I can get to some classes and try to fix (mend?) some relations (Craig and Loren and I had talks).

February 24th, 1956 - Dear Diary, I went to the Cedar game tonight. They beat us. I danced practically all night with Claude. I can't figure Craig out.

February 25th, 1956 - Dear Diary, I went to a show and dance tonight with Craig. The "Sweetheart's Ball" was girl's choice, but the show "The Outlaw's Daughter" wasn't.

February 26th, 1956 - Dear Diary, I went to church today and tonight. Craig gave the scripture in meeting. Fireside was at his place tonight.

February 27th, 1956 - Dear Diary, I have got to get busy again, this time with signs. I am in charge of about a dozen things.

February 28th, 1956 - Dear Diary, we had a "Treasure of Truth" night in M.I.A., but it was too short of a class.

February 29th, 1956 - Dear Diary, if I sing in the Solo-Ensemble, I will have to get a song learned, maybe "The Kiss" finally. I walked to Glendale to practice. I practiced the play in town until 12:00.

March 1st, 1956 - Dear Diary, I was too sick today to even stay up. Oh, what a time! I guess I've had too many out late nights. I made it for "Dark Wind," thanks to Dale.

March 2nd, 1956 - Dear Diary, I stayed home tonight for a change. Our plays went fine! I wrote to Mark.

March 3rd, 1956 - Dear Diary, it was a usual Saturday today, but I didn't get much done. I feel too feeble.

March 4th, 1956 - Dear Diary, I have enjoyed this Sunday. Chick and Jean came over for a while. I bore my testimony in meeting.

March 5th, 1956 - Dear Diary, it's too darn bad!! There were three boys who got drunk Friday. Some people can't keep their word. Jeremy (again), Ellis, and Vance.

March 6th, 1956 - Dear Diary, in M.I.A., we had a ward music festival. We sang. Craig was the only boy. Bless him. I gave a talk.

March 7th, 1956 - Dear Diary, somebody goofed! Today was the Solo-Ensemble. No – I didn't even go. I'll learn! (maybe)?

March 8th, 1956 - Dear Diary, Wendy came home tonight. It seems really good to have her again.

March 9th, 1956 - Dear Diary, we girls have been painting all day and cleaning house. Wendy and I went to a skit, a building fund program. I wrote for it.

March 10th, 1956 - Dear Diary, we nine went to church. It seemed good. I had fireside up here tonight. Mr. Rose gave a wonderful talk about testimony.

March 12th, 1956 - Dear Diary, it seems like there are so many things to do. I made candy and popcorn for the Senior sluff fund.

March 13th, 1956 - Dear Diary, we had a Junior Gleaner Comradery tonight. Nights like this are to remember.

March 14th, 1956 - Dear Diary, I practice at noon to learn "Wild Irish Rose" for Saturday.

March 15th, 1956 - Dear Diary, I stayed after school tonight to help decorate for the Seminary Prom, "Let the Sunshine in."

March 16th, 1956 - Dear Diary, tonight I stayed home. I didn't have a way to the dance. Mr. Christensen probably forgot me.

March 17th, 1956 - Dear Diary, tonight Luanne and I both sang in a banquet program.

March 18th, 1956 - Dear Diary, I went to three meetings today and to Kanab to practice singing for the festival. Some of us hope to go to Salt Lake City.

March 19th, 1956 - Dear Diary, it took persuasion, but finally "Dark Wind" will go to Dixie. Gwenda is taking Carolyn's place. (She wouldn't).

March 20th, 1956 - Dear Diary, the cast practiced then saw the show (after school), "A Star is Born." Oh, it was good. We girls really cried!

March 21st, 1956 - Dear Diary, time flies by. There is so much to plan and get ready for. Events are scheduled from now on.

March 22nd, 1956 - Dear Diary, the cast stayed up late tonight practicing for tomorrow. I'm glad we finally decided to take it.

March 23rd, 1956 - Dear Diary, we took "Dark Wind" to Dixie today for the speech festival (lots of fun)! Tonight was the yearbook carnival too.

March 24th, 1956 - Dear Diary, Luanne and I went to Cedar with Mr. Rust this morning. We saw "Ill Trovitore" (grand opera) and spent the day with Wendy.

March 25th, 1956 - Dear Diary, I have been tired all day, but this week has sure been worth it.

March 26th, 1956 - Dear Diary, this weekend, we Seniors go on our "educational tour" to Salt Lake. We are busy with plans.

March 27th, 1956 - Dear Diary, we had a good M.I.A. tonight. Daddy wrote me a $15.00 check. Bless him!!

March 28th, 1956 - Dear Diary, we have been busy all day and late tonight. Oh boy – tomorrow at 6:00 a.m.

March 29th, 1956 - Dear Diary, here we are in Provo, Robert's Hotel, room 75. We have been to the mental institution. Oh, what a place. We have been to B.Y.U. campus. We learned a lot. We saw "Never Say Goodbye."

March 30th, 1956 - Dear Diary, Salt Lake City, Maxum Hotel, room 336. We went to Primary Children's Hospital and visited six campuses. Very nice. Phoned Clarrisa and Dandy and saw Ken. Went to the show "Anything Goes."

March 31st, 1956 - Dear Diary, we went to the zoo this morning. Mrs. Hanes and I shopped this afternoon. I was tired. I manipulated a phone call to Thomas. He sounded so good (I'm still silly). I went on a date with a boy named Bob. Rose and Richard arranged it. Saw "Mr. Roberts" and "Rebel without a Cause." They were good shows. I'm tired tonight at 2:14 a.m. (or morning).

April 1st, 1956 - Dear Diary, the trip has been wonderful!!!!! We went to the tabernacle broadcast. It was very good. We started for home, tired and ready to see the country again, but – oh, what fun it was!!!

April 2nd, 1956 - Dear Diary, I wouldn't have missed it for anything! Safe and sound, home again, except I feel all in! They were happy to see and hear from us again. Mighty Seniors back to school.

April 3rd, 1956 - Dear Diary, I had to stay home today to recuperate, I guess. Not quite used to it, or I've just caught a germ. Oh, well. I'm not a bit sorry I went. I'm thankful I got to go.

April 4th, 1956 - Dear Diary, we had a party for Roger today. He is quite a cook. He made his own birthday cake. There was an assembly for F.H.A. Prince Charming.

April 5th, 1956 - Dear Diary, it is Girls' Day tomorrow. I am not asking a date. About everyone is chosen. Besides, who would I ask? I am busy as usual.

April 6th, 1956 - Dear Diary, Girls' Day and night was fun. A group of us Senior girls had a fun time, dancing (every set), and partying (at Phyllis') until 2:30.

April 7th, 1956 - Dear Diary, the Bishops and the Cornellias cooked our suppers tonight out at Liddy's Canyon. It was a lot of fun. We were making up for Easter. I sure like them.

April 8th, 1956 - Dear Diary, it seemed good to teach my baby class again. It is like spring. Blossoms are budding.

April 9th, 1956 - Dear Diary, we have the hot water installed (gas), finally. I worked on Yearbook today and tonight.

April 10th, 1956 - Dear Diary, I led the singing in M.I.A. tonight. It has been a long time. Rita has a plan for this summer.

April 11th, 1956 - Dear Diary, we finally finished the yearbook. The last section is sent in. Oh boy!

April 12th, 1956 - Dear Diary, tomorrow night is our last class dance, our formal Senior Ball. Our theme is "Moments to Remember."

April 13th, 1956 - Dear Diary, our dance wasn't a very successful one, as far as making money is concerned and the number there.

April 14th, 1956 - Dear Diary, I cleaned house today, as usual. It seems good to have hot water without making a fire.

April 15th, 1956 - Dear Diary, I went to preparation meeting in Fredonia. Luanne and I sang "The Morning Breaks" in meeting tonight. Her mother helped us.

April 16th, 1956 - Dear Diary, I am going to ask Mrs. Haynes if she will make my graduation formal. I mean, I hope we can afford one.

April 17th, 1956 - Dear Diary, no one went to M.I.A. Me and my folks don't get along all the time like we used to. Sometimes they can't understand how I feel.

April 18th, 1956 - Dear Diary, there was a deal Jenny almost got me into. Thank goodness Craig (brother) and Mama reminded me where I belong.

April 19th, 1956 - Dear Diary, we Seniors have 50 or more poems to collect for Speech class. I'm glad. We need it.

April 20th, 1956 - Dear Diary, tonight was the Junior Prom. I had fun. It was a very nice dance! "In a Little Spanish Town" was the theme. Ikie was my date.

April 21st, 1956 - Dear Diary, I cleaned house today, as usual. I made some pies and did some ironing. Tomorrow is stake conference in Kanab.

April 22nd, 1956 - Dear Diary, today and tonight has been wonderful. We sang in the choir and had some very good meetings. Tonight's M.I.A. program was something to remember. It was testimony. I bore mine, so did Nathan, Jim, and Darnell (three new missionaries).

April 23rd, 1956 - Dear Diary, we Seniors had a party tonight in Alton Canyons. It was really fun, even if we did run into mud and flat tires. Four of us girls went with Dale.

April 24th, 1956 - Dear Diary, if there is a will, there is a way. I manipulated (after quite a time) to get to the Junior M. Men and Junior Gleaners party in Kanab tonight. I'm glad I did.

April 25th, 1956 - Dear Diary, we are busy copying 50 poems for Speech and learning songs for graduation.

April 26th, 1956 - Dear Diary, today we were all shocked to learn Jack Crofts was killed at the saw mill.

April 27th, 1956 - Dear Diary, tonight was the Post Prom. I didn't have much fun, except I danced with Darnell. Yes, he was with Rose (of course).

April 28th, 1956 - Dear Diary, I am going to Henderson to work for Aunt Valoyce as soon as school is out. I'm glad I have at last found out.

April 29th, 1956 - Dear Diary, I read in "The Doctrine and Covenants" today in the blooming orchard. Tonight I went to Glendale to meeting. The Seminary presented a program.

April 30th, 1956 - Dear Diary, Mama and Daddy went with some Glendale women to a funeral in New Harmony. I sang "In the Garden." Daddy prayed. We saw Wendy. I have my formal cloth.

May 1st, 1956 - Dear Diary, I stayed down after school to type and see about my formal. Mrs. Haynes is making it. I went to M.I.A.

May 2nd, 1956 - Dear Diary, all the chorus is making pink blouses alike for the festival. We are busy with graduation songs and chorus songs.

May 3rd, 1956 - Dear Diary, this afternoon we saw the show "Home in Indiana." We liked it.

May 4th, 1956 - Dear Diary, we (chorus and band) presented an assembly. Then the B.Y.U. did. The yearbooks are here.

May 5th, 1956 - Dear Diary, I went to Cedar today to the music festival. We really had a good time. This is another day to remember.

May 6th, 1956 - Dear Diary, Wendy was home for a while. It seemed good. She is enthused about doing things here, and I am enthused about leaving. I finally wrote to Mark again.

May 7th, 1956 - Dear Diary, I have a cold still and again. We did pretty well at the festival, I believe.

May 8th, 1956 - Dear Diary, I didn't get to M.I.A. tonight, so I finished my poems. We are all busy signing yearbooks.

Dear Craig

Time is going by.
We soon must leave Valley High.
Then we say good bye to friends.
The fun and companionship ends,
But still in all of our hearts,
Friends ever have their parts.

Craig, when times are sad,
And life's sailing seems quite bad,
Think then of your friends, those who care.
You'll remember life is fair.
If you're blue, remember too
They think a lot of you.

Life is worth living
When it is full of giving.
Help another his burden to lift.
You will feel your own troubles shift.
If you are true to what's right,
Blessings are in sight.

May you win success
And always happiness find
In all the high goals you have set.
And please, in the years to come
Don't entirely forget.
Cathy

To Luanne

Friend of mine, lovely and with dignity pure.

CATHY CORNELLIA

A flower blooming has nothing more.
Possesses no more of beauty or grace,
Looking upward – has no sweeter face.
Your smile on face and lip,
Cheers and brightens.

Such talented fingers play music so moving
All cares find gentle soothing.
Friend, with voice so fine,
When I hear your song divine
I thrill at its richness and meaning.
It echoes in my heart
And deep feelings start.

Memories of inspiring times spent with you
Shall ever enlighten what is true.
Such a sensitive spirit as you possess
Will always find contact with holiness.
Be then, friend of mine, ever sweet and true.
Love, achievement, and happiness will ever shine on you.
Cathy

To Rita

Friend, only a few more days
Then we go different ways.
Memory shall linger in my heart,
Though we must part.

Friend, I remember through all the years,
Through the smiling and through the tears,
You have always been there
To encourage, cheer, and share.
To help me dare.

Friend, unselfish and sweet,

My Dearest Diary

You make friendships complete.
There is one who always can be true.
Dear, it is you.

Friend, in time of need, when blue inside,
In you I can always confide.
May I ever find this bond?
Of you I am more than fond.
Dear, I love you.
Cathy

May 9th, 1956 - Dear Diary, the Seniors are busy preparing for graduation, leaning songs and marches. Today was V-day. We painted "56."

May 10th, 1956 - Dear Diary, tonight was Seminary graduation. Our class received special certificates. It was a nice program.

May 11th, 1956 - Dear Diary, Ikie had a party (15th). I went with some kids to a practice for graduation at Mrs. Lamb's, then to the show in Orderville. I got home by 12:00.

May 12th, 1956 - Dear Diary, I have an awful sore throat. I wonder if I will be able to sing Friday. Trust my hard luck (or silliness). We had a candy pull tonight.

May 13th, 1956 - Dear Diary, I taught my class for the last time. I went to Sunday school for the last time (for a while anyway).

May 14th, 1956 - Dear Diary, I stayed home today to see if I could recuperate. Just think, only a few days more, then school is out for good (for all Seniors).

May 15th, 1956 - Dear Diary, Phyllis is married! So is Lorna Gale. It must be catching.

May 16th, 1956 - Dear Diary, the days are passing very fast. Our days are filled with practicing, writing in yearbooks, planning, talking, thinking, but no studying.

May 17th, 1956 - Dear Diary, we did some practicing and didn't have much school. Jenny and I stayed afterward to make decorations.

May 18th, 1956 - Dear Diary, tonight was our graduation. A time never to be forgotten.

May 19th, 1956 - Dear Diary, I came to Henderson, Nevada tonight. I am awfully tired.

May 20th, 1956 - Dear Diary, I went to Sunday school and meeting and a fireside. I met the Thompsons again and the two boarders.

May 21st, 1956 - Dear Diary, I love this family already. I'm going to like it here. I went with Fane T. to some shows in Vegas.

May 22nd, 1956 - Dear Diary, I went with them (Fane, Bill, and Sharon) to a ballgame in Las Vegas. I made some cookies. Bill asked. I like Roy.

May 23rd, 1956 - Dear Diary, I went with Roy to the lake. There were five of us. I am really burned.

May 24th, 1956 - Dear Diary, I scrubbed today. I went with Fain to graduation and a party afterwards. I got better acquainted with Edwin and Donna.

May 25th, 1956 - Dear Diary, I washed today. I went to Las Vegas with Fain. I went shopping this evening. I wrote letters tonight.

May 26th, 1956 - Dear Diary, I ironed today.

May 27th, 1956 - Dear Diary, what a day. I'll have to tell you sometime. I have made it to church though (and fireside).

May 28th, 1956 - Dear Diary, I washed today and ironed some. I went to M.I.A. tonight with Bill and Sharon and a new roomer (Richard).

May 29th, 1956 - Dear Diary, I have been cleaning house. I played ball today with Sharon's group.

May 30th, 1956 - Dear Diary, I made three pies and cake today. We had a picnic in Boulder Park. It is very pretty there.

May 31st, 1956 - Dear Diary, we have been bottling apricots. I sure am tired. I work and am kept busy with kids (I love them), meals, etc.

June 1st, 1956 - Dear Diary, I went to some shows with Fane tonight. He is quite a guy. I haven't decided what to think of him.

June 2nd, 1956 - Dear Diary, I washed today, etc. Richard paid me a compliment. Roy makes frequent Utah trips.

June 3rd, 1956 - Dear Diary, it has really been a good Sunday today. I enjoyed the meetings.

June 4th, 1956 - Dear Diary, we had fun tonight at an M.I.A. party (progressive party). Thanks to the boys who live here.

June 5th, 1956 - Dear Diary, Leland and Ruth keep me running, so does the cooking and cleaning and washing and ironing. It isn't too hard.

June 6th, 1956 - Dear Diary, I went with Fane to some more shows, usual place. I am getting to like him more than I thought I would. Oh, oh.

June 7th, 1956 - Dear Diary, today has been tired and busy. It is Leland's 3rd birthday. Aunt Valoyce hopes the baby comes right soon.

June 8th, 1956 - Dear Diary, I washed today and made a cake and meatloaf. Richard left. Aunt Valoyce is to stay in bed. We are wondering about a can in the fridge.

June 9th, 1956 - Dear Diary, Aunt Valoyce had a baby girl early this morning. We have been to the hospital twice. They won't let me see her. The baby is darling.

June 10th, 1956 - Dear Diary, we went to church today. The kids acted up in meeting. I went with Fane to fireside. He has been up home. He saw the folks.

June 11th, 1956 - Dear Diary, I am tired tonight. It can be a handful. Roy reminded me about M.I.A. too late.

June 12th, 1956 - Dear Diary, Aunt Valoyce and the baby came home today. The kids (and I) were glad to see them.

June 13th, 1956 - Dear Diary, some of the ladies gave Valoyce a surprise gift-party. It was very sweet.

June 14th, 1956 - Dear Diary, I went with Fane again. I have got to, as Lincoln says, "watch myself." We differ every once in a while (Fane and I). He is still too wolfish.

June 15th, 1956 - Dear Diary, the water has been off all day, so I washed tonight. I finished about 9:15 or so.

June 16th, 1956 - Dear Diary, we have been cleaning and resting today. Ike came to dinner. We took him home afterward.

June 17th, 1956 - Dear Diary, I went to Sunday school and meeting and with Fane. He prayed in church. After work (at 10), we went to the dam. It is pretty at night. He has helped me a lot, I believe.

June 18th, 1956 - Dear Diary, Roy and I made it to M.I.A., though we were late (as usual). Bill and Roy tease a lot. They wonder about Fane.
   He told me of his plans, for him and Jan, Bill, and Sharon's apartment. I finally got him to treat a meal.

June 19th, 1956 - Dear Diary, I have another job lined up (lucky me) for July. So I will be here for a while. Bill has moved out. I might go home for the reunion.

June 20th, 1956 - Dear Diary, Bill and Sharon are to be married tomorrow in St. George temple. They seem so young, 17 ½ and 20 (I think).

June 21st, 1956 - Dear Diary, I went with Fane (after some manipulating) to the reception (he thought I had left). It was a nice one. Six of us got away from the others. Later, Fane and I went into Vegas. We walked down Fremont St. He did some shopping for me. He gave me a necklace.

June 22nd, 1956 - Dear Diary, I rode the bus from Vegas to Hurricane tonight. I am at Uncle Steven's. Alma and Diane are here too. I am anxious to see my folks tomorrow.

June 23rd, 1956 - Dear Diary, we all met at Moccasin today (Lynn is with Wendy). We had a big picnic, took pictures, visited, and had a program in the church. I will be going back Sunday or Tuesday, I think.

June 24th, 1956 - Dear Diary, my plans have changed. Too much has happened. Mama is still sick (mostly tired from being sick). She has had pneumonia. The doctor said she is to take care of herself. She needs rest. Eva Blackburn has died with the flu. I went to her funeral today. One never knows.

June 25th, 1956 - Dear Diary, yesterday, Mama finally broke down and asked me to stay with her. I can't go back now, now that I understand how things are at home. I phoned Aunt Valoyce. She can manage.

June 26th, 1956 - Dear Diary, well now I am to be home. I left everything but sleepers, two dresses, and shoes down there. Rather a sudden change of plans, huh? But it must be for the best.

June 27th , 1956 - Dear Diary, Edward C. died today. He has been sick with heart troubles, and he was an old man. What a wonderful person he is.

June 28th, 1956 - Dear Diary, I'll have to get used to being home. A month away can make things strange. Wendy and Lynn are in love. They are together a lot of the time.

June 29th, 1956 - Dear Diary, I went to the ranch today. The boys are there. We are trying to remodel, and boy are things in a mess. I am needed.

June 30th, 1956 - Dear Diary, I went to Brother C.'s funeral. We all will really miss him. I keep thinking of Jenny and how she must feel.

July 1st, 1956 - Dear Diary, I went to Sunday school, meeting, and fireside (with Lynn and Wendy). It is going to take a while to stop thinking of Henderson and those down there. Yes, I miss Fane. We both wondered if I would.

July 2nd, 1956 - Dear Diary, I got my clothes today. Aunt Valoyce sent them up with LaVar.

My Dearest Diary

July 3rd, 1956 - Dear Diary, I went to a dance tonight. Sam and I rode down with Lynn and Wendy. I spent most of my time talking on the bench.

July 4th, 1956 - Dear Diary, the program was very nice this morning. I went to the rodeo with Guard, Rose, and Rita. I went to the mutton supper tonight (all of us went, including Dennis and Collin). I saw the show "On the Waterfront."

July 5th, 1956 - Dear Diary, Mama and I have been painting the kitchen yellow today. It was a job, and we were tired from last night.

July 6th, 1956 - Dear Diary, we (Bishops and Cornellias – C and C) met the Bullocks (S and M) at the ranch tonight. We had a good party then went to bed. The ranch is different now. It will never be like it was years ago. Things have to change.

July 7th, 1956 - Dear Diary, this morning we ate breakfast at Navajo. We sure like the Bishops. Chick and Jean met us there for a few minutes. It was good to see them. We all left again. We came home through Main Canyon.

July 8th, 1956 - Dear Diary, I went to Sunday school but not to meeting. Daddy didn't get back in time. I read for a while.

July 9th, 1956 - Dear Diary, we are remodeling, and how! It is a mess, but oh, we are glad to be doing it at last. I went to Kanab with Rita.

July 10th, 1956 - Dear Diary, Aunt Cora and Uncle Leo were killed in a car accident this afternoon.

July 11th, 1956 - Dear Diary, I have been painting all day. The kitchen is all painted and the wall paper is up. I went to a shower for Virginia and to the show "The Robe."

July 12th, 1956 - Dear Diary, we have us a new fireplace in the living room. I am going on the mountain with the 4-H. I am to be queen of the 24th!

July 13th, 1956 - Dear Diary, today was the funeral. It was certainly a big one. It was held in the high school gym. It was very nice. We went to their home afterwards.

July 14th, 1956 - Dear Diary, I have really cleaned today. It has needed it badly. There has been plaster and paint besides dirt.

July 15th, 1956 - Dear Diary, we (our class) held a class in the hall of the new building. We were the first ones. Our class is too big for the bishops room. We went to church and fireside.

July 16th, 1956 - Dear Diary, Mama, Mary Ann, and I went to St. George with LeAnn, Arvilla, and Eva. We had a good visit with the folks. LeAnn and I went shopping.

July 17th, 1956 - Dear Diary, we had a fun M.I.A. party in the old party place above the bridge. I made a cake and punch. I went up with Luanne and Ramona.

July 18th, 1956 - Dear Diary, did I tell you? Sunday, I and my six attendants for the 24th had our pictures taken. I have been sewing on my yellow dress.

July 19th, 1956 - Dear Diary, I am helping with a 4-H group. I wrote them a skit. We had a meeting. Tonight, Mama and I went to "Demetrious and the Gladiators."

July 20th, 1956 - Dear Diary, I went to town today and practiced 24th songs, "Utah Star of the West" and "Indian Love Call." I visited with Virginia.

July 21st, 1956 - Dear Diary, we have been house cleaning and ironing. Wendy went with Lynn to the Grand Canyon. We had a talk about it.

July 22nd, 1956 - Dear Diary, Daddy talked in church tonight. We had fireside at Rita's tonight.

July 23rd, 1956 - Dear Diary, I have been in town most of the day getting ready for tomorrow, practicing, making a float, and such things.

July 24th, 1956 - Dear Diary, I was queen for the day. It was an experience to remember. I won in a talent show with "Indian Love Call." It was a fun parade.

July 25th, 1956 - Dear Diary, we are tired from yesterday. Mary Ann and I went on a walk. I went to an M.I.A. leadership in Alton. I still don't know what's going on in Mutual.

July 26th, 1956 - Dear Diary, I wrote a letter today (to Fane). I had said I would send an earring. I told him thanks too. I hope he understands.

July 27th, 1956 - Dear Diary, I went to 4-H today. We planned for our trip to the mountain. I have been painting the living room pink.

July 28th, 1956 - Dear Diary, I have been cleaning house all day. Lynn is having dinner here tomorrow.

July 29th, 1956 - Dear Diary, Lynn had a birthday (24th) dinner with us. I went with Donald to fireside, and afterward we had one of our long talks. We are friends who understand each other.

July 30th, 1956 - Dear Diary, I painted more pink today. The bathroom is about finished.

July 31st, 1956 - Dear Diary, I and my three 4-H girls went to Duck Creek today. We were bothered with boys, a snake, a porcupine, and cold weather.

August 1st, 1956 - Dear Diary, today we had some silly, but fun, laughing times, a long hike to ice cave, and our skit night. We have plenty of neighboring campers.

August 2nd, 1956 - Dear Diary, chaperoning a club can have its problems, but it is still fun. We had handy-craft today.

August 3rd, 1956 - Dear Diary, what a day! Things were rounded up. We came home in the afternoon and went to "Deep in my Heart." Oh!! It was good.

August 4th, 1956 - Dear Diary, we cleaned house today. I went to Aunt Orvilla's and helped her. Then tonight I stayed at Aunt Eva's with the kids.

August 5th, 1956 - Dear Diary, we've really had a day! Sharlene and her folks came out. We had a good afternoon. I stayed with the kids again and visited with Helen.

August 6th, 1956 - Dear Diary, I came home this morning. Eva and Neldon are back from Henderson. Lavar is awfully sick.

August 7th, 1956 - Dear Diary, we (Wendy and I and Lucille) went to Kanab today. I got some shoes and lipstick. Guess who we saw? Yes, and he talked to us. That's another dream I must wake up from.

August 8th, 1956 - Dear Diary, I am running the fruit stand this week. Roger is at the ranch. It gets rather monotonous.

Dreams #1

Dreams can be wonderful things.
And dreams can be mistaken and sad.
In dreams you can always create new scenes, views, loves, and feelings.
Many dreams I have had.

Dreams can carry you for miles,
Either forward now or backward then.
It's wonderful: these new eyes that see
And these feelings that feel all over again.

Dreams build and create anew.
Maybe you can make new colors or shades;
Set a new goal to strive for and reach;
Find new density to brooklet and still glades.

Dreams can take you from right here
To new lands of experience far away.
But dreamer, remember in most dreams it's sweet,
May seem complete, but you cannot stay.

Dreams open lands of fantasy.
You feel you would like to leave awhile?
You will find your mind is wandering,
as you think of flower or a lover's smile.

In dreams a new love can live. Be watchful, dreamer.
Are you choosing a live model and dreaming higher?
Yes? Dream 'til he's perfect.
He'll set you afire.

Dreams can make dreamers foolish.
Reality and dreams can differ.
You must become fully awaken.
If dreams blind your vision

You'll be mistaken.

Dreamer be careful with dreams.
It is sad to wake from a dream you dreamed was true, sweet reality.
Measure the worth of dreams
Not, "It ought to be."

Dreams can be wonderful things.
Though they are kept in fantasy land,
Can't forget their loveliness and value.
And remember in dreams, ideas are planned.

August 9th, 1956 - Dear Diary, Wendy is staying home from work. She has a bad cold. I was at the fruit stand all day.

August 10th, 1956 - Dear Diary, Mrs. Lamb is sick in bed. I did not know about it until I went to practice. I am at the fruit stand still.

August 11th, 1956 - Dear Diary, I worked in the fruit stand again today. It was about the best day I've had.

August 12th, 1956 - Dear Diary, the Bishops and Cornellias went to Cascade Falls and Cedar breaks. Keith is down for a few days. It was a fun trip. Then I went to meeting with Keith (though we were late). I like him. He is going to Finland on a mission.

August 13th, 1956 - Dear Diary, Mr. and Mrs. Bishop, Keith, and I went to Zion Park tonight. It was raining and nice. Keith had never been there. Then we went to picnic in Kanab. It was really a good show. Those Bishops are quite the people!!!

August 14th, 1956 - Dear Diary, I went to M.I.A. tonight. There were only six people there (just us girls). Claude came in and asked me if I had fun. I said yes. He left.

August 15th, 1956 - Dear Diary, we (the two families) and Natalie had a fun corn roast and melon bust and weenies at the lake. Claude didn't come. He has his troubles. Darn it. We had fun playing kick the can and visiting.

August 16th, 1956 - Dear Diary, I went with the Bishops (except Claude) to the sand dunes. Keith made the date (by phone), but I can bet his folks schemed as usual. Oh, it's fun. We ate melon. Keith and I went to "Target Zero" in Kanab. I may never see him again, and we know it (I think), but just the same -----.

August 17th, 1956 - Dear Diary, Mama, Mary, and I went with the folks to Salt Lake today (Keith went back to Payson) for the reunion. We stay at Aunt Clarissa's. It seems so good to see all of them again, Heber, Sandy, Lorraine, Lena, Clarissa, and Grandpa.

August 18th, 1956 - Dear Diary, we had the Jackson reunion today. I hope I always remember it. We all met in Fairmont Park. We had a good singing, talking time! I've learned a lot today and tonight.

August 19th, 1956 - Dear Diary, well, here we are home again. What a week!! I wish there were more like them, but I'm tired tonight. We came home with Sandy and Barbara. It's hard to say goodbye. It's sure good to see them.

August 20th, 1956 - Dear Diary, I've really got to get on the stick! Only ten more days until the fair. "The Kiss" has got to be learned. Thank goodness I can walk to Emily's.

August 21st, 1956 - Dear Diary, I walked to Glendale today to practice my song. I had a good visit this morning with Helen. I got a permanent tonight.

August 22nd, 1956 - Dear Diary, I went to Kanab today to have my picture taken for the queen contest.

August 23rd, 1956 - Dear Diary, I have been wondering how Craig is getting along.

August 24th, 1956 - Dear Diary, those are quite the practices I have at Amy's. It seems that and the fruit stand and helping on the house is all I do.

August 25th, 1956 - Dear Diary, today Keith left for New York. Now he is on his own. Good luck to him. He'll be a fine missionary.

August 26th, 1956 - Dear Diary, I went to Hurricane this afternoon with the Bishops. I had my hair cut. I like trips with them.

August 27th, 1956 - Dear Diary, today was a usual day, practice, fruit stand, and house work.

August 28th, 1956 - Dear Diary, I went to Kanab today to practice "walking on stage" for Thursday night. I sang for Loretta. She can get up only a few minutes.

August 29th, 1956 - Dear Diary, today I went to Cedar for a swimming suit, slip, and shoes. I got some of my shopping done. Thank goodness for the $45 check from Aunt Valoyce.

August 30th, 1956 - Dear Diary, tonight was the contest. It was very frightening and exciting. I will remember it for a long time. I sang "The Kiss" (finally).

August 31st, 1956 - Dear Diary, tonight was the coronation. No, I didn't win anything, but it was an experience to profit by. I made some new friends too! Yes, Tom was there. I wonder if I will always feel a little something for him, though I know I should forget. Remember a year ago?

My Dearest Diary

September 1st, 1956 - Dear Diary, I got a letter from Keith yesterday. He was in New York. He sailed the 28th. Guess what!? Fane is married!! I thought anytime he would come to see me. Life must be like that!!!

September 2nd, 1956 - Dear Diary, this is a day to remember. Wendy and Lynn are engaged. Isn't it wonderful! It has really been a day. An extraordinary Sunday.

September 3rd, 1956 - Dear Diary, Marion and Valoyce came out today. It seemed good to see them again. Oh, I have a lot of memories! Memories to forget. What if I had really cared?

September 4th, 1956 - Dear Diary, I felt a little lonesome today as the school bus left me behind. I remember it left other Seniors too. I busied myself with sewing.

September 5th, 1956 - Dear Diary, I sewed today too. Tonight was a reception. I hope they are happy. Why does it even bother me? I'll feel better soon. It was probably just a little shock.

September 6th, 1956 - Dear Diary, Mama and Aunt Orvillia have been doing corn all day. I sewed as usual. Rita came up to visit for a while. It was good.

September 7th, 1956 - Dear Diary, I went to Cedar today to shop some more. We went to Jeanette and DeRoy's reception. It was very nice.

September 8th, 1956 - Dear Diary, I sewed all day today and still have a mess to do over.

September 9th, 1956 - Dear Diary, Craig came home today. He goes back tomorrow. Craig, the same as ever. There's something I must forget, feelings, I guess I knew.

September 12th, 1956 - Dear Diary, Wendy and I have been sewing. I have been helping bottle and pick apples.

September 13th, 1956 - Dear Diary, Mama, Wendy, and I saw "I'll Cry Tomorrow." It was really good. We've been sewing again and still.

September 14th, 1956 - Dear Diary, I got a letter from Keith today. I'm glad he wrote again. I have been sewing all day.

September 15th, 1956 - Dear Diary, I cleaned house today. It's time I was. The house is in a mess, and there are three batches of ironing.

September 16th, 1956 - Dear Diary, I sang in meeting tonight. They asked me this morning. I received my Senior Gleaner award. We had a very good fireside.

September 17th, 1956 - Dear Diary, we had a party at the lake tonight, Bishops, Cornellias, Bolenders. I wonder, will this be the last of its kind? I will have a lot of memories.

September 18th, 1956 - Dear Diary, Mama, Mary Ann, and I went on a walk today to Minchee, and we went in Bear Hollow.

September 19th, 1956 - Dear Diary, I came to C.S.U. today to start college. Uncle Marvin and Aunt Valoyce brought me over. I sure like the kids and Mrs. Romaver. Our room is 19.

September 20th, 1956 - Dear Diary, Wendy is so busy with meetings. I am alone most of the time, so I went to Jean's and downtown, and I cleaned in the dorm.

September 21st, 1956 - Dear Diary, we went to an assembly this morning and filled out cards. There was a dance tonight. A "get acquainted" for Freshies. I didn't get much acquainted (with the guys I mean).

September 22nd, 1956 - Dear Diary, oh, what a day! We Freshies registered about all day. It is really an experience. We were treated to a show tonight.

September 23rd, 1956 - Dear Diary, this is another day I'll remember. My first Sunday at C.S.U. church (Institute) has been wonderful. I have met more kids. Some boys have been up today. They ate our cake. I have mixed up feelings too. Am I homesick? Maybe a little.

September 24th, 1956 - Dear Diary, today the Sophomores registered. Tomorrow we start classes.

September 25th, 1956 - Dear Diary, today was my first day of school at C.S.U. We had a "get acquainted" dance in M.I.A.

September 26th, 1956 - Dear Diary, I think this is all going to be a bit different. Oh, I must not let anything muddle much.

September 27th, 1956 - Dear Diary, college days at last! What will they bring?

September 28th, 1956 - Dear Diary, the dance was fun. Tonight was the game with Dixie. They beat us by 21 points. I really have a cold. I sang in Parowan.

September 29th, 1956 - Dear Diary, I worked today for a Mrs. Higby. Thank goodness. I have prospects for work.

September 30th, 1956 - Dear Diary, I stayed in bed most of the day to recuperate. Tonight was a really good meeting. Ron M. gave a wonderful talk.

October 1st, 1956 - Dear Diary, Humanities is quite a class. I like it for more reasons than one. I tended kids twice today.

October 2nd, 1956 - Dear Diary, I sang in M.I.A. tonight so did Wayne (he is darling). I had fun. I danced with Lane M.

October 3rd, 1956 - Dear Diary, I sang in Relief Society today. I sang for Mr. Johnson. I don't know what to sing for opera tryouts.

October 4th, 1956 - Dear Diary, tonight was the Lambda Delta Sigma rush party. It was fun, but some weren't there.

October 5th, 1956 - Dear Diary, almost everyone went home today. I almost got lonesome. Wendy is at Snow College. We had a real fun A.W.S. party at the ranch tonight.

October 6th, 1956 - Dear Diary, today Wendy and I have been here together. We have listened to conference, written letters, and made a cake.

October 7th, 1956 - Dear Diary, I sure do like Humanities! I am lucky not to have any bad classes.

October 8th, 1956 - Dear Diary, M.I.A. was really good. Mr. Felt is teaching "Courtship and Marriage" lessons. There was dancing afterward. I didn't stay.

October 9th, 1956 - Dear Diary, today we had Freshman initiation with green letters, socks, frizzy hair, and all.

October 10th, 1956 - Dear Diary, we had more initiations today. I pledged Lambda Delta Sigma tonight. I was up by 6:00 again and got breakfast. We also had our Freshie assembly.

My Dearest Diary

October 11th, 1956 - Dear Diary, today was the last of the initiation. We had some more chain dances, etc. There was a game today. We won too. Wendy, Steven, and I went to the show.

October 12th, 1956 - Dear Diary, I went home with Sharlene today. We really had a time, blind-dates and all. We saw Yvonne Cornellia Burr.

October 13th, 1956 - Dear Diary, today has really been a day. We went to conference in Dixie, came home, and got in on some church here.

October 14th, 1956 - Dear Diary, we have some manipulations in this apartment. I wish I could learn from them. I need to learn lots of things yet.

October 15th, 1956 - Dear Diary, we saw a show in M.I.A. tonight. I had seen it twice. It was "Oliver Cowdery."

October 16th, 1956 - Dear Diary, guess what I did? I am now on the paper staff. Why? Because I am interested! Ron is editor.

October 17th, 1956 - Dear Diary, tonight was Lambda Delta Sigma. We went to meeting then to the show "Trapeze."

October 18th, 1956 - Dear Diary, tonight we were supposed to try out for opera parts. We are waiting again.

October 19th, 1956 - Dear Diary, Wendy and I came home tonight. It seemed so good. We went to the Deer Hunter's Ball and saw the kids.

October 20th, 1956 - Dear Diary, Mama, Wendy, and I have been together today. Everyone is happy and well. It seems so nice here again. We had home-evening.

October 21st, 1956 - Dear Diary, Craig is home too. Today it was almost like old times, yet so different.

We came back to Cedar.

October 22nd, 1956 - Dear Diary, tonight we had our first opera production meeting. It lasted a while too.

October 23rd, 1956 - Dear Diary, I finally met, rather, he finally met me, tonight. Wayne had never seen me before. I have seen him.

October 24th, 1956 - Dear Diary, I went to another paper meeting tonight. I sure think a lot of the editor!

October 25th, 1956 - Dear Diary, Annette, Carma, and I left Lambda Delta Sigma early tonight (in spite of the party) for opera production again.

October 26th, 1956 - Dear Diary, we Freshies (a few of us) have been making our float for Homecoming. It is now after 1:00 a.m.

October 27th, 1956 - Dear Diary, today and tonight was Homecoming: assembly, game, parade, and dance. Something to remember!

October 28th, 1956 - Dear Diary, today has been outstanding! We have gone to three conference meetings. They were just what we needed. I hope I remember. I hear Wayne would like a date.

October 29th, 1956 - Dear Diary, they have asked me to be a Relief Society teacher. Goodness! I hope I can!

October 30th, 1956 - Dear Diary, I am really going to like our M.I.A.s at the institute.

October 31st, 1956 - Dear Diary, I am so thankful I am here! I like it, and the people are wonderful.

November 1st, 1956 - Dear Diary, Mama, Daddy, and Mary Ann came to see us today. I had just written a letter home when I met them coming up the stairs. It seems good.

November 2nd, 1956 - Dear Diary, I tended kids tonight. Later, Wendy and I went to Jean's and had a visit with Mama and Mary Ann. Mama is getting her teeth lined.

November 3rd, 1956 - Dear Diary, Wendy, Mama, Mary Ann, and I all went shopping today. It seemed so good to be with them. Dolly's folks were here too.

November 4th, 1956 - Dear Diary, what a day!! It has been an extraordinarily good Sunday. I gave the talk. Wayne asked me. We had our first Relief Society.

November 5th, 1956 - Dear Diary, yesterday Wayne gave such a good talk!! "Beauty is more than skin deep." I was so proud of him. He is an officer in Sunday school. Guess what? He took me home! I sang in church too. He is wonderful (and I drove his car).

November 6th, 1956 - Dear Diary, we had a good M.I.A. tonight, but there were some who were not there.

November 7th, 1956 - Dear Diary, I made it to part of the paper meeting tonight. We sure have some silly ones.

November 8th, 1956 - Dear Diary, I sang "My Friend" over Cedar T.V. tonight. It was quite an experience. Ron really complimented me. Oh thrill!! He looks just as good as he sounds.

November 9th, 1956 - Dear Diary, we went to Dixie on the bus for the game. They won again. I had a good visit with Rita. It was good seeing her again.

November 10th, 1956 - Dear Diary, we saw "The King and I." It sure was good.

November 11th, 1956 - Dear Diary, today has been another good Sunday. I gave my first Relief Society lesson. We also had the program in meeting.

November 12th, 1956 - Dear Diary, there is plenty to do. Things keep us busy. I wonder just what this week will hold!?

November 13th, 1956 - Dear Diary, M.I.A. was good tonight. Lately all (most) of the girls have been finding dates for Friday. I wonder if I dare. It is a little different from high school.

November 14th, 1956 - Dear Diary, I am writing a poem on Thanksgiving for the paper. I hope Ron will like it. Wayne is sure hard to locate.

November 15th, 1956 - Dear Diary, I finally got a date with Wayne. I asked him to the dance for tomorrow. We kids went to the concert (after Lambda Delt) and Utah symphony at Mark Aubrovenell. Wonderful!!

November 16th, 1956 - Dear Diary, the Intersociety Ball was tonight. Oh, it was really a time to remember. My date with Wayne was all I had hoped it would be. I really like him. He sure is cute.

November 17th, 1956 - Dear Diary, everyone slept late this morning. After last night, we are sleepy. We cleaned house. Sharlene and I went to some shows with Aunt Rua and Uncle Ivar. It is a noon eclipse.

November 18th, 1956 - Dear Diary, we had some good meetings today. I led the singing in Sunday School. I sang "My Testimony" in a meeting at Canaraville. I haven't had much time home.

My Dearest Diary

November 19th, 1956 - Dear Diary, we are all anxious to go home again. We need to too. There are many things to do. We are kept busy and tired.

November 20th, 1956 - Dear Diary, Ron really likes my poem. He keeps telling me. Oh, it makes me glad. I wrote it hoping he would like it.

November 21st, 1956 - Dear Diary, Wendy and I went home with Lynn today. It really seemed good to see him again. Wendy has been needing to. It seems so good to be home again. Mama and I have been really cleaning.

November 22nd, 1956 - Dear Diary, we have sure had a nice Thanksgiving. Most of Daddy's folks came over for dinner. We had close to 40. I went to the dance on the bus and saw some of the kids again. I miss Craig.

November 23rd, 1956 - Dear Diary, it seems so good to visit with loved ones again. Lynn showed us some films. We saw Lincoln in one of them - England, Holland, Rome, and others. He has seen a lot. Aunt Clarissa and family are here. Oh, it was good.

November 24th, 1956 - Dear Diary, I had a very good visit with Luanne today.
   I sang in a banquet "Suddenly There's a Valley." Then Daddy took Luanne and me to Gerald's farewell party. I have had such a nice time home. In a way, I want to stay longer. Oh, I love my loved ones.

November 25th, 1956 - Dear Diary, we came back today at 5:30. It was late when we got back. We went to Sunday school at home. Everyone (almost) was home for the holiday. Then we all said goodbye again. Last year seems a long way away.

November 26th, 1956 - Dear Diary, well, back again. I did my washing and some catching up on a few things.

November 27th, 1956 - Dear Diary, tonight I went to opera practice. I don't know why. It didn't do me any good, but I did write three missionary letters. I am writing to Mark again.

November 28th, 1956 - Dear Diary, I tended kids tonight. I got 75 cents. It will help a lot. I am broke. Katherine and I have been Relief Societing today. I was late for paper meeting. Ron was the only one there. Ron writes poems too. Oh, I'm glad.

November 29th, 1956 - Dear Diary, we had so much fun tonight. After Lamda Delt, we (Relief Society) had song practice and work meeting. We made some very pretty candles and balls.

November 30th, 1956 - Dear Diary, for dilly! The dance was the "Harvest Ball." Wendy was queen. Pete and I had fun just sitting and acting awfully silly. I would rather be silly than sad.

December 1st, 1956 - I have been alone today. Everyone (of my roommates) is home or on a trip. I have accomplished quite a lot. I have been needing to.

December 2nd, 1956 - Dear Diary, I am so proud of Wayne today! He was in charge this morning. It happens we are in the same class too. I like him.

December 3rd, 1956 - Dear Diary, I get so behind. I can't seem to catch up. There is something all the time. We all are so tired.

December 4th, 1956 - Dear Diary, we went to M.I.A. Wayne went this time. There was dancing afterwards. I goofed and didn't get to dance. Oh, I feel in an awful mood!!!

December 5th, 1956 - Dear Diary, I have studied for hours but still there is more. It is Pete's birthday. We went to "Messiah" practice.

December 6th, 1956 - Dear Diary, tonight was Lamda Delt and the tree lighting program. I want to remember this night. Ron was there. There was a party, and it has begun to snow.

December 7th, 1956 - Dear Diary, the snow is so beautiful. I love the campus in winter, snow on the pines. Deanna and I walked to Uncle Bud's to get some milk and Mama's letter.

December 8th, 1956 - Dear Diary, today I wrote a poem, and we made candles. Tonight Pete, Wendy, and I went to the basketball game. We won the tournament.

Four Loves

Four loves along their way were fairing.
One day they met, loves comparing.

The first love grew as a flower.
It was opening, sweetly into bloom.
Away fled all gloom.
It waited with patience two years ere it might be picked,
For then it would be full blown;
Open, ready where love shown.

The second love was as a flame.
It had been started as a kindled spark.
In a few years, hark!
The once little flame, being nourished, had grown into a bright fire
Clear and strong.
Yes, it would burn true and long.

The third love always was boiling.
It could bubble and be right nice and warm.

It had lots of charm.
And a number knew it and received a glow.
Then each one wanted love to return.
It made each of their hearts yearn.

The fourth love was as a new food.
It was not very easily understood.
Tasted, it was good.
It was planned to be a nice meal, but in storage.
It waited to be thawed out,
Wanting to be cared about.

Four loves along their way a fairing
Someday true love will be sharing.

December 9th, 1956 - Dear Diary, we have had such a nice Sunday. I love Sundays and its meetings. I thought I might be home, but no. I wrote home instead. I am happy.

December 10th, 1956 - Dear Diary, Sharnell and I sang "Oh, Holy Night" in a club meeting tonight. We saw Ron at a K.S.U.B. office. Wendy and I went to a violin concert by Ricu. It really was impressive.

December 11th, 1956 - Dear Diary, tonight was the M.I.A. Christmas party. We saw the film "How Near to the Angels," and Santa came.

December 12th, 1956 - Dear Diary, I am almost finished with my Institute picture of the "Iron Rod." Ron came down as I was finishing. We went to paper meeting. Tonight was "Oklahoma." It was really good.

December 13th, 1956 - Dear Diary, we took tests in Lambda Delt tonight. Then we hurried to Messiah practice, went to the game for a while, then studied.

December 14th, 1956 - Dear Diary, tonight was the Christmas Ball. No, we didn't have dates, so we stayed home and studied and sent cards and letters and went to bed for a change.

December 15th, 1956 - Dear Diary, today we slept and cleaned house, ate, caught up on washings and ironings, and studied a little. We enjoy Saturdays.

December 16th, 1956 - Dear Diary, we went to our meetings. Lynn came this afternoon. Sharnell and I sang "Oh Holy Night" in meeting.

December 17th, 1956 - Dear Diary, we are having tests in all classes. Oh, what a time. I have worked on a report about all day and night.

December 18th, 1956 - Dear Diary, it is dead week. Thank goodness. We are just to stay home and study for tests on the 'morrow.

December 19th, 1956 - Dear Diary, we came home tonight. Classes lasted only part of the day. Lynn, Wendy, and I went shopping first.

December 20th, 1956 - Dear Diary, it seems so good to be home again. We sleep as long as we want and are free from study worries.

December 21st, 1956 - Dear Diary, the first night here, Wendy and I went to a Valley ballgame. Last night, we went to the chorus program. Today, I went to school to visit. It seems changed.

December 22nd, 1956 - Dear Diary, we cleaned house today and did some baking and candy making. School is out for the kids.

December 23rd, 1956 - Dear Diary, I went to the new church for the first time. It seems so different, almost like another town or something. It is nice.

December 24th, 1956 - Dear Diary, we went to the Christmas program. I miss Lincoln tonight. I hope he is ok. Wendy and I stayed up late. Next year she won't be here.

December 25th, 1956 - Dear Diary, it seems good to be here. With Lincoln's picture on the mantle, we are all home around the fireplace. I feel a little vacant. The kids are happy. I am glad. I did not go to the dance. I am home.

December 26th, 1956 - Dear Diary, I got a card from Donald this morning. It makes it harder. Why must I think of the past? It is done. I guess he doesn't want me to forget. I will (if I can).

December 27th, 1956 - Dear Diary, we had a class reunion tonight. Only a few were there. It was fun (and funny) as always.

December 28th, 1956 - Dear Diary, it seems so good to visit with Mama again. I hope she can have good health again. I wish the boys were more considerate.

December 29th, 1956 - Dear Diary, tonight and today has been full of memories for me. Things can change so in a year. Tonight we had a ward reunion.

December 30th, 1956 - Dear Diary, it seems so strange going to the new church. The dear old one is coming down. I lead the singing in church tonight.

December 31st, 1956 - Dear Diary, we had an ice cream party tonight. I went to the dance with Amy. I visited with the kids. Tonight I feel a bit lonesome. I wonder how 1957 will be. We go back to school tomorrow. I miss the kids there.

Memorandum

Dear Diary, the year of 1956 has meant a lot to me. Graduation was a highlight. Then there is college. It is really a change full of experiences. Most of the time I can honestly say I enjoy college. But, as you know me, you will remember I have interests and dreams of various kinds. Yes, I am the same person who began writing years ago. I am eighteen. Soon I will be nineteen, then I will be in my twenties. Though years change and hasten by, I will always remain Cathy.

"What do you think the future holds?" you ask. I do not know exactly. But I know my own dreams. I know what I want. I will remember life has its ups and downs. They are necessary.

Some ideals are closer than before. I must learn how to touch them. Maybe I shall hold them one day. Faith and patience I need to remember.

This dear book of memory is to be a treasure. Silly? Sometimes it may be called so. Good for a laugh, a tear, to recall something I had almost forgotten, to remind me of "those days."

So, I close this book, knowing what it has meant to me, knowing it shall mean even more.

Dear Diary, the time has come to bid you a fond goodbye and a thank you for what you have meant to me. So goodbye, Dear Diary, I'll treasure you as ever.

Sincerely,

Cathy

2009

May 29th, 2009

We were married May 29th, 1959.
It has been 50 years today!
We can't believe that many years have gone away.

Each year seems to go fast,
As a river goes to sea.
One of these years our lives will into eternity.

Always, Mark and Cathy Pine

I still can't believe we have been married 50 years! The years seem to pass faster and faster. How fun it was to see our grandkids again. It was a very special occasion, being with those we love and seldom see. How grown up they seem. How talented. How smart and successful. I wish it could have lasted longer. Reunions are very important and worth the work, time, and money. I hope everyone feels that way. I hope we thanked them enough. I hope they know we love them. Our six children and their dear spouses worked so hard and did so well with planning and performing and getting it all together. It was a beautiful, memorable time!

GLOSSARY

4-H: An in-school and after-school youth program which focuses on hands-on projects.

Aaronic Priesthood: A lower level of priesthood in the LDS Church available to worthy male members of the church beginning at age 12.

Baptism for the Dead: A religious practice in which living people are baptized as a proxy for people who have died without being baptized.

Conference: Generally, a gathering of members of The Church of Jesus Christ of Latter-day Saints that takes place twice a year in Salt Lake City, UT. There are also stake and ward conferences.

Endowment: A ceremony in the LDS church that includes making promises to God and receiving blessings.

F.F.A. (Future Farmers of America): A youth program that focuses on Agricultural education.

F.H.A. (Future Homemakers of America): Now called Family, Career and Community Leaders of America, it is a youth program that focuses on Family and Consumer Sciences education.

Farewell: In the LDS Church, a church meeting where new missionaries speak before they leave for their mission. Friends and family may also host a farewell party for the missionary.

Institute: A religious education program for college-aged members of the LDS church.

M.I.A. (Mutual Improvement Association): A weeknight activity hosted by the LDS Church for teenagers.

Patriarchal Blessing: A blessing given by a priesthood holder in the LDS church to church members, which may include insights into the person's life and future.

Primary: A program for children under the age of 12 in the LDS Church.

Relief Society: The organization for women in the LDS Church.

Road Show: A set of skits that were performed by ward actors for other wards within their stake by traveling to each audience's location.

Seminary: A religious education program for high school-aged members of the LDS church.

Stake: In the LDS Church organization, several wards make up a stake.

U.E.A. (Utah Education Association): Public schools would often have an early release or day off during the U.E.A. convention once a year.

Wards: Congregations within the LDS Church in which members from a geographic area attend worship services together near their homes.

The Y: A café that was located where two highways met, forming a "Y" shape.

Made in United States
Orlando, FL
07 February 2024